Demons and Familiars

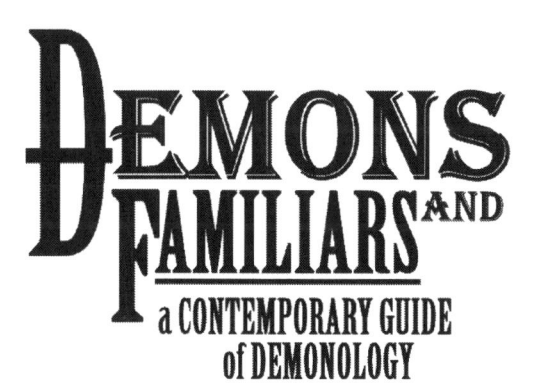

DEMONS AND FAMILIARS
a CONTEMPORARY GUIDE of DEMONOLOGY

Copyright © 2017 by Melinda K Lyons

All rights reserved. No part of this publication may be reproduced, distributed, or transmitted in any form or by any means, including photocopying, recording, or other electronic or mechanical methods, without prior written permission of the publisher, except in the case of brief quotations embodied in critical reviews and certain other noncommercial uses permitted by copyright law. For permission requests, write to the publisher, Melinda K. Lyons at the website below.

DEMONS AND FAMILIARS:
Written & Edited by, Melinda Kay Lyons
Self-Published with Kindle Direct Publishing

ISBN: 13:9781979509725

Illustrations:
Original Cover Art Copyrighted by, Hektor2
Interior Illustration of Chapter Eight by, Carolyn Lyons
and a range of other artists.

Anchorage, AK
Official website:
http://www.Lastfrontiermedium.com

*True power comes from lifting
the veil of illusion. Embracing love as your Source
and Light as your guide.*

Contemporary Guide Use and Counsel

What you are about to explore is a range of dynamical elements and strategic origins of the supernatural. It is strictly inadvisable nor ethical to solely remote view it's nature and habitual traits if one is in the desire to fully comprehend these diabolical entities. Demons and familiars not only *do* exist but are fully *aware* of your reading this text and or intentions in the past, present and future transitions. What you do in the *now* with the information is exceptionally crucial and will have a sizable impact on you and others. Do unto others as you would yourself with the exception these don't get to you first. It is in the personal responsibility of the reader to note and understand these entities do not take words, intentions, and thoughts lightly. Advising to proceed with caution in the knowing this device is meant as a handbook of sorts when in the suspicion of a Demonical presence. Be warned of the tolerance it may take an individual to stomach what you may be impressed with and or about to read, experience and or endure.

The intentions of the written guide is to allow a chance for even the most innocent of individuals hope in being able to debunk and or identify what he or she is undergoing. It is not recommended to take matters into one's own hands unless is considerably experienced spiritually/ metaphysically and or possesses the innate ability to discern the divine differences between a *benevolent* spirit, or a *malevolent* one. Beholding the vade mecum of Demonology and it's familiars in lengths of further educating, enlightening and to embark on the fruit of knowledge. But tread with caution for this document alone does not constitute sure protection, and or a guarantee that all who may identify the predator may be granted the wisdom or the knowhow in extracting the super powerful oppressor.

The credibility in this text is considered professional based on the author's experience independently as a near-death experiencer, Demonologist and Psychic Medium, including previously reported claims by countless clients seeking peace from the diabolical disturbance.

CONTENTS

Chapter One
THE UNIVERSAL ARENA
1

Chapter Two
IDENTITY and APPEARANCE
35

Chapter Three
ADVANCED ABILITIES
51

Chapter Four
COSMIC ORIGIN vs RELIGION
67

Chapter Five
THE MALEVOLENT TYPES
91

Chapter Six
KNOCK KNOCK:
INFESTATION
121

Chapter Seven
THE DISTURBANCE BEGINS:
OPPRESSION
147

Chapter Eight
INFLUENCE and POSSESSION
175

Chapter Nine
THE ULTIMATE POWER to FREEDOM
201

THE MAKING OF DEMONS and FAMILIARS
233

ACKNOWLEDGEMENTS
247

ABOUT THE AUTHOR
249

Chapter One

Universal Arena

LIFTING THE VEIL

The cognitive notion that there is nothing beyond what is physically tangible promotes further illusion of the incomprehensible universe. Humanity coexists between two realities and each realm of reality dwells on opposite sides of the spectrum that is considered 'truth'. Truth of what is real and what is not -fact vs myth. Right now, physically you are living the matrix that is considered to the collective, a 'fact' but in reality it is myth, or better to say, *partial truth*. The collective base of consciousness on earth live through the five senses: touch, taste, sound, smell, and sight. Unfortunately, the majority suffer amnesia of the sixth sense of the human consciousness. This particular sense presumes one obtaining the ability to engage in psychic talents, gifts or to say the, *God Sense*. This ability is what allows most to use what is commonly called, intuition -which in fact is a psychic ability that is now labeled as the common phrase, 'gut feeling'. Besides listening to the gut instinct as a helpful guide in where to go or what to do, it has been known to aid in discerning the divine difference between energy frequencies. Between positive and negative vibrations that tend to clash amongst the other in a spiritual sense -metaphysically.

You are *in* a physical body that is in fact 99 percent empty space that is vibrating in a high velocity that is invisible to the naked eye. The human anatomy is about 60 percent water whereas the hydrogen only counts for 11 percent of that water mass. Though water consists of two hydrogen atoms for every oxygen, hydrogen has much less mass. Concluding that 93 percent of the mass in the human body is stardust. Why? Because stars are made of exceptionally hot gas that is primarily hydrogen and helium, which are the two lightest elements. Stars get their shine by burning hydrogen into helium in their cores then later in their lives create heavier elements. In these findings, we, the human race are not separate from the galaxy and what it embodies. We are the same in all that surrounds us, being created as well as interconnected by the number one element that can never be destroyed -*energy*.

Everything in this world was born out of vibration, each creation maintains a certain frequency, vibrating in a unique way individually. What is physical and metaphysical are of different frequencies and vibrations for nothing is without its own vibrations in the over one hundred *billion* galaxies in the observable universe. Everything has its own vibration. A tulip has its own frequency while a rose has too it's own energy frequency. Animals to different minerals, to even tables and chairs, shoes and mountains all possess their own frequency. But what brings humanity to own the name 'unique' is the ability to be able to change and shift our frequency freely without struggle. It is human emotions that grant the consciousness the stupendous ability to adapt and change to its own feelings causing one in continuous resonance to one's consciousness at all times. We have the ability to resonate with everything in the universe and can give and receive energy.

And these emotions determine the type of energy one is more likely to reside in energetically.

There are two energies in the close to incomprehensible universe: *positive* and *negative*, (light vs dark, love vs hatred). Positive and negative energies vibrate at different levels of frequency causing one to be able to discern the difference with the power of intuition and or other Psychic abilities. Like living humanity where there are positive people (love) and negative people (hate), metaphysically (spiritually) there too consists of the same energies (spirit, souls, entities).

The power of emotion through the human consciousness guides one to undertake a shift in awareness and in energy. When one experiences the emotion of joy the energy transforms into a lighter vibration that may crystalize into an effortless construction of positivity. Energy alone whether positive or negative creates what it embodies emotionally, consciously. Negative emotions will also construct itself into the feelings one conceives by developing into its opposite, creating a destructive configuration. All that exists whether physical or metaphysical always attracts and brings itself to what it resonates with energetically, but cannot be done without one's thoughts that brought the emotional data to fruition.

All emotions within the human consciousness cannot be birthed without the seed of thought. And these thoughts are what creates the emotions that then create the either positive or negative energies one resumes in the present moment. All emotions come from a thought, and these thoughts reside within all that are consciously aware of thyself in the present moment whether physically or metaphysically. None need be aware of the energy resonance for it to appear as so, for all in the universe that is energy shall blend into its emotional guidance whether fully conscious of the happening or not. Humans possess the emotional guidance in order to predict the energetic outcome and with the help of this system we are granted the rare opportunity to shift into whatever vibration we consciously choose in the moment. No other level of creation has this gift.

Words whether positive, or negative, energy cannot help but give the equal equivalence to the vibrations the words carry. Water for example, has been scientifically proven to change shape based on a delicate study on words and emotions and environmental placement. Words and phrases that are based on universal truths, like *love, thank you* and *appreciation* will crystalize water into pleasing symmetrical hexagons. However, water that has been exposed to negative words or phrases, such as *you idiot, ugly, war* or *moron* will produce misshapen undistinguished crystals. After careful analysis, science has been able to prove the significant effects words can have not only on water, but towards the human consciousness. Hardening the consequential outcome of one's decision to reside more so on the positive or negative side of consciousness through thoughts that create the emotions, thus enabling the energetic equivalence. Thoughts become things within this universal balance. Everything meets with what resonates with it -whether positive or negative in vibration.

Considering this, we can establish the divine gift of free will for each level of creation including those that are physically and metaphysically conscious in the universe. Being able to distance the positive vibration that is love from what is negative and hateful embarks the idea one may perceive that each is to decide their own fate energetically by the course of one's free will.

Life as we know it comes with blessings as accompanied with the curse that which brands the equilibrium of all things. The universal balance that allows everything to have its own opposite to engineer and maintain the surplus of energy operations.

We live in a world that consists of laws such as the law of gravity while in the metaphysical world (the other side, afterlife) there are too laws of its own. And to some of these laws requires each individual a level of understanding and deep awareness in order to appeal to these laws willingly. No dimension comes without a law of its own for all in the universe are interconnected on a continual basis forevermore. Each dimension allows different levels of consciousness to journey through their level of understanding and lessons that which graduates each to new heights.

Where there is positive thoughts (emotions) there are positive dimensions, and where there are negative thoughts (emotions) there are negative dimensions due to the consciousness resonating with the said vibrations. Each level of thought is charged by an energy frequency and these frequencies morph and adapt in harmony with those thoughts. But these thoughts that are charged by exceptional amounts of passion and or desire, triggers the universe to only harmonize more with those thoughts and emotions. The rhythm of the universe forces every human being to form thought-habits which harmonize with the dominating influences by the dimension thus continuing the cycle of previous thought patterns. So to say, when a person is focused on positive thoughts that are gathered by emotions and passion -this enables correspondence to the thought frequency that is emanating out into the universe. The universe cannot help but give back what we think, feel and or believe with passion. When this happens, we then enable the universe to also shape our environments that will thus only force the feelings and thoughts to proceed. This is the same for negative thoughts that are too charged by an exceptional amount of passion and or desire.

Because this is so, we are forced to remember the significant impacts thought patterns, words spoken, and emotions can have on a conscious being.

To understand the energy vibrations and it's origins, is to likewise grant the reader a chance in looking into the cosmic and intelligent nature of Demons and it's Familiars.

Negative energy as well as positive energy live in the minds of people. One-half of every atom of physical matter and every unit of mental and physical energy occupy all humans. Where there is light there is darkness (absence of light) and where there is goodness in people there is the capability of committing pure evil. (absence of love). To understand, the human consciousness (soul) consists both of negative and positive energy, but thanks to the blessing of the *Universal Law of Free Will,* we are given the rarity to choose which one to reside in more. However, there are defiant beings that condemn those that possess their absence, seeking to defile this cosmic order and of humanity.

The repulsion towards humans is undeniable as soon as one encounters such an abomination. They possess no empathy for any sentient being whilst carrying exceptionally acute intent to overtake and control. Fear is their biggest ally when contacting, the physical world in order for them to impose the *four steps* of malevolent activity. Each entity invades the human consciousness by planting fear into each human they focus on. Feeding into the minds of their victims the most dreading of thoughts, images and sounds and emotions, in hopes it will charge them to leap to their own death or cause harm to others they love. No human is exempt from experiencing the close to intolerable terror these forces impress on the chosen victim. Not even a 'saved' person in Christian or Catholic belief are untouchable. Any, and *all* souls no matter the religion, or lack thereof, is not without risk of becoming a potential target.

Through great animosity demonical beings are capable to break down the person's free will in order to partake in the final stage. Once the victim's free will has been broken considerably, the entity then may attempt the most malice strategy of all, *Possession*. It is advisable for one to tread cautiously through the valley of the shadow of death for the knowledge one gains, comes a shellshock of it's true authenticity.

They will manifest in nearly countless of ways that is sorely underestimated by the human race for centuries. Fully comprehending the true power these entities possess, would only demonstrate a darkened tunnel that never sees the light of day while being consumed from the invasion of your worst fears imaginable -then multiply that by *ten thousand.*

All who dare to challenge this *primary evil* is warned of the serious naivety one will be humbly reminded of when cornered by such inhumane spirits. They strive purely to cause pain and suffering, finding joy in the cry of your infant child. Finding disgusting pleasure in leading your dog to find fear in you without being aware. While laughing in the course of the battle for sanity over madness as you continually doubt your own judgment. These things live to make one's life a living hell. They take pride in bringing you to your lowest points of personal destruction as you scream in dismay and confusion. It is noteworthy when considering the emotional land slide one may face after the preternatural horror intensifies on a physical and psychological scale, making even the toughest of men to cower in the dim lighted hallway. Casting even the brightest of souls, rays of defeat and doubt, but are not without the beam of resolution and freedom from this spiritual suffering.

THREE OF THE UNIVERSAL LAWS

FREE WILL

The universe consists of many laws and these laws are what allow the course of the energies in the cosmos to evolve and adapt overtime. We abide by these laws whether one is aware of them or not and none are without living by the nature of the laws.

Although there are a considerable amount of laws that are yet to be discovered, there are at least three laws that impress the most profound impact on humanity. These three laws are what gather the confirmation of what will be in the course of time after a certain amount of energy is charged to allow these laws to take action definitely. All of what is energy that exists abide and resonate with each law effortlessly without strain on the universe.

In order to calculate the likelihood of an individual to come into contact with an inhuman spirit, would be by influencing the energies by the use of Free Will. This Universal Law is interchangeable and is not to be limited to only those of this physical world. All who are created by energy -which is inevitably everything and everyone are too impacted by the *Universal Law of Free Will*. This particular law states that, *any sentient being that possess (that is) a consciousness (soul) is thus given the undeniable opportunity to choose what they will. A universal freedom within one's own consciousness -the gift of full leverage of cause and effect. This law permits any and all levels of consciousness to make any choice one wills itself without any difficulty on the universe and other laws.* It is a law that is a part of you and I. It is inside of you, and can never be taken away, nor could it ever be stolen, nor borrowed without also your free will choice to consent so, or to give in by one's choosing. We are always given the choice no matter the cause and effect from before us. Free will is what is and always will be you consciously within the existence of what *is* energetically existing. There is no other better freedom than the Universal Law of Free Will. But when one is willed with such a precious gift, one is also handed the full extended issue of consequence for one's bold, and to some degree -blind decisions.

With the explicate ability to make free will decisions this enables all energies in possession of a full consciousness to choose which frequency one will harbor in. The human body and consciousness is constructed in both positive and negative energy frequencies which entices the humans link towards either positive or negative behavior. And these behaviors are encouraged by the thoughts that grow from within the human mind that are energized by emotions. We are *both*, both with the capability to be loving or hateful, to be self-sacrificial or murderous. With this understanding, one is then able to comprehend this next step towards enlightenment of cosmic truth.

Because of the Universal Law of Free Will most humans are longing with desire of something more than what they are given. Longing for that one thing they cannot have but are urging with a thirst for further taste of adventure, reassurance, comfort, and or exhilaration. The freedom of either asking or taking, to earn or to steal unjustly. And sometimes, one may be asking for something more than they had bargained for, more than they were prepared to endure. It's a natural trait in the human to start to learn the power of curiosity and to then begin the desire to explore that which they are curious about. And although the person may be in the strong belief that they are ready for what they wish for with the freedom of choice, doesn't necessarily mean they are indeed. As that old but powerful saying goes -as true today as it were the moment it were originated: *Be careful for what you wish for.*

Some will go to great lengths by choosing to do things that are well intended and or selfish in nature. Some will decide to do something with extraordinary caution, whereas another may most likely be reckless in their decision making while letting the possible outcomes slip through the cracks of the filter in one's mind. And it is in these moments of one's thought patterns where one should consider the odds that would lay ahead depending on one's choices. This is exceptionally true for those that choose to connect with the metaphysical level by personal decision, that is when one is opening the door to another reality.

INVITATION

The willingness to gain communication with a departed loved one is something most can relate to within reason and empathy, but not always are we going to agree on ways of *how*. It is more socially accepted that when one wishes to communicate or speak to a loved one that is departed, is to do so in prayer or through spiritual counsel. Well versed spiritual aid can bring a certain degree of relief to those that are missing their loved ones, and although some may long for more, they usually will accept and proceed in life with gratitude. But some are not as satisfied with that lesser amount of communication and will take matters into their own hands.

In the *Law of Invitation*, it is understood that *any and all who choose to summon someone, something, or have an experience with a willful invitation -whether physical or metaphysical, is translating a declaration of absolute certainty of what one is desiring in the universe energetically.* This thought that is charged by the energy and emotion of desire, will have a follow-through from that which one is inviting. The universe goes based on the laws of resonance and whatever one is residing in internally, based on thoughts that are too charged by emotions, those emotions then trigger within the waves of communication out into the universe. And that level of communication in energy is then transmitted and is received through the powerful streams of frequency causing that which one desires to have no choice but to eventually match and manifest.

With this law in motion the universe cannot help but bring forth what one is focusing on or wishing to experience with an open invitation. Every law cannot help but do what it was designed to do. No matter what, we are bound by these laws because it is how it was designed since the dawn of creation. In the Law of Invitation, the universe cannot help but organize everything into motion with such immaculate precision in order to manifest that which one is inviting into their life consciously. This is something that one must take with great caution or else suffer close to irreparable damage to one's psyche and or ones current emotional, physical condition.

The Law of Invitation goes beyond what most would consider reasonable or realistic for those that experience the outcome to this are left with a spiritual scar. This law is not to be limited to only the products of our environment but to take note this law takes form upon the coexistence of those physically incarnated or metaphysical beings in the universe. However, when one decides to make this declaration of invitation: whether by projecting images and visualizations within one's mind, or by speaking these desires out loud verbally -the universe will have no choice but to respond undeniably without question.

To speak plainly: The Law of Invitation effects everyone and everything physical and metaphysical. What one chooses to desire within their consciousness, whether fully aware of it or not will have no other choice but to eventually come into that desire from the open invitation willingly. This is not to be taken lightly. Any, and all who willingly choose to open themselves energetically, and or physically to entities on the other side are only awaiting a supernatural molestation of the peace.

ATTRACTION

Based on the information laid out regarding the Law of Invitation, there lies the one law that allows this to come into motion: the *Law of Attraction*. The Law of Attraction entails that *whatever one focuses on consciously or subconsciously that is supported by a considerable amount of passion (that is created by thoughts and emotions) will drive that focus into manifestation.* This law is exceptionally delicate and precise due to the amount of energy it takes to accumulate that which one is focused on. Whether one is focused on something they do or don't want, doesn't matter to the universe for it is what you (the conscious individual) is concentrating on.

The universe doesn't care whether you are a good person or a bad person. The universe doesn't decide what is meant to be manifested or not, it only goes based on what the consciousness is focusing on with again, a considerable amount of *passion*.

Passion is what drives the attraction into effect. Passion is derived from the emotional database of the person, whether positive or negative, it will entice the universe to respond. It doesn't matter to the universe if you want it to happen out of good emotion, or if one is focused on something with extensive fear and or worry -causes the law of attraction to take affect nonetheless.

Like attracts like. What this means is the universe correlates to what it generates, and what we consciously generate in our thoughts and emotions that charge negative or positive energy frequencies, we *create that reality by attracting it.* Whether one wishes for something, or worries over something, the universe will bring that into manifestation.

Everything in the world is created by positive and negative vibrations but the significant difference between humanity and trees, flowers and the rest of the universe is we we're given the gift to *discern*. We were gifted with a free will that allows us the choice to choose the thoughts and or desired experiences into our life.

THE LAW RELATIONSHIP

The said laws correlate in a bond that is unavoidable no matter how one may attempt to evade it. You cannot experience one law without the rest responding to the other due to everything in the universal working. There is a mirror effect happening in the course of now, and what is to come, whether one is aware of this happening energetically, or not. The universe is based on thoughts and the thoughts that are chosen in the moment are what is to come in the near or later future definitely.

Freedom to choose with the power of thought and emotions are granting the universal consciousness the ability to drift from one energetic trigger to the next. Which thought one chooses is up to the holder of the thought based on the emotions the holder of the thought carries. But due to the *Universal Law of Free Will*, the two fellow Laws that follow - *Invitation* and *Attraction,* carry with them the outcome of those thoughts and emotions. The *holder* of his or her thoughts is the commander of the chosen reality one perceives or permits in his or her consciousness. However, it does not exclude to the extent of the physical reality of such commands.

The realm of physical density inhabits all things that are energetic -including those that are invisible to the naked eye. It is in this intimate cosmic relationship that which constructs our mental, emotional, and physical realities to its absolute potency. Although the knowledge of this pure conscious wonder is indeed great, can it also become the holder's worst nightmare if not tailored and honed with a considerable amount of wisdom or practice.

Power through thought is so often abused and underestimated today as it was centuries prior, but is not to be misunderstood as dangerous. Consciousness in the universe is only detrimental to the safety of the holder and others when one is watering the contents of their mind with little to no caution to how it shall sprout.

Each Universal Law requires a specific energetic frequency that can only be summoned by the holder's consciousness (emotions, desires). It is the responsibility of the holder to understand their power to make things happen and manifest. And it is within the power of the holder to choose what one *invites* to experience or not with the *free will* that thus *attracts* that which one is desiring.

THE ENERGETIC EXPERIENCE

Everything in the universe embodies its own vibrational type of energy, whether that energy is positive, negative, or neutral. All in the cosmos has a way of existing that is always in motion and that motion enables the conscious being or material item to make its mark in this realm and others.

There are two kinds of energies in the universe -Light and Dark energy. *Light* energy refers to the kinetic energy carried by electromagnetic radiation, a subset of electromagnetic spectrum, that which is visible to the naked eye. Energy is higher as we move up in the frequency spectrum known as Light. This energy is responsible for the sense of sight. Light energy is energy that can be seen and used to see the matter around us. It can be manmade or natural, like the light from the sun. Whereas *Dark* energy in physical cosmology and astronomy, is an unknown form of energy which is hypothesized to permeate all of space, tending to accelerate the expansion of the universe. This hypothesis is the most accepted when explaining the observations since the 1990's that indicates the universe is expanding at a rapid rate.

Quantum physics says that as you go deeper and deeper into the workings of the atom, you see that there is nothing there – but only energy waves. Indicating an atom is something like an invisible force field -like a tornado, which emits waves of electrical energy. We are made up of atoms. And atoms are continuously giving off, and absorbing, light and energy. Continuously happening -even during sleep state. Every cell in the body has its atoms lined up in such a way that it has a negative and a positive voltage (frequency/ vibration), inside and out. Every cell in the human body is like a miniature battery. Each cell has 1.4 volts of energy – not much, but when you multiply by the number of cells in your body (50 trillion) you get a total voltage of 700 trillion volts of electricity in your body.

We are all created of atomic energy waves, and because it is impossible to separate waves for we are all connected, our energy waves are always meeting and getting entangled in each other. The result of such invisible interactions we call 'good vibes' or 'bad vibes', depend on whether the other waves we meet are in-synch with us or out-of-synch.

It is in this scientific finding we are given not only an energetic but divine ability to detect a supernatural (energetic) shift. As we are all connected energetically so are those on the other side of reality. As you are borrowing your human body, you are also given an innate ability to discern the energetic difference between a benevolent entity or a malevolent one thanks to our energy heritage. There you will discover the intricate commonalities and links based on the body's reactions and responses to certain energy types that make contact with yours -whether the energy belongs to a living human, animal, or a supernatural (metaphysical) presence.

THE ENERGETIC RESPONSES

The energetic vibrations are going to have a significant impact on the human body as well as their emotions, images subconsciously and consciously along with their mood and or reaction types.

For example, those that come into contact with a benevolent entity like an Angel, or an Ascended Master like Jesus Christ, or Buddha, they will commonly feel a sensation of love, security, compassion, empathy, non-judgment along with a strong sense of peace and tranquility. However, those that are met with malevolent entities will experience negative sensations like hate, fear, guilt, high levels of anxiety, greed, resentment and or pain from previous memories flooding into their image filter of the consciousness. These are significant differences and can be easily identified when given the opportunity to carefully analyze one's body, thoughts, emotions, and feelings when in the presence of an unknown entity.

The ways to tell the energetic responses vary depending on the entity that is present, but most commonly are reported to be what is listed below. The list is not to be limited to only what is confirmed, but is to be used as a guide towards further validation, and or confirmation to the energetic reactions people most commonly experience.

RESPONSES TO BENEVOLENT SPIRITS

MIND/ EMOTION/ INTUITIVE RESPONSES
- Inspiration
- Affirming thoughts and or images
- Positive telepathic confirmations
- Unconditional love
- Empathy
- Tranquility
- Joy
- Reassurance
- Happiness
- Security
- Relief

- A strong sense of safety in your home or current location, emotions, etc.
- Divine guidance
- Absent of fear
- Absent of worry
- Absent of doubt
- Contagious optimism
- May experience dreams that bring absolute peace and supreme comfort to your presence

BODY AND ENERGY RESPONSES
- Fully energized in body and soul
- May sense a healing sensation
- May sense a positive yet soft tingling sensation in self entirely
- Serenity and peace will overcome your whole being granting absolute certainty of the encounter being positive
- May suddenly be absent from physical pains
- Sudden unspeakable calming to your whole body granting elite solace
- Have suddenly been cured from an illness and or other medical or psychological diseases/ cancers

Although Benevolent beings will permeate positive vibrations, as one encounters these precious entities, one must also be in the knowing of what it may be when in contact with its opposite.

RESPONSES TO MALEVOLENT SPIRITS

MIND/ EMOTION/ INTUITIVE RESPONSES
- Sudden fear
- Sudden anxiety
- Overwhelming doubt
- Overcome by negative emotions brought on by sudden memories, and or pains
- Nightmarish experiences whether asleep or physically awake that overtake all thought
- Sudden outburst of anger
- Sudden bursts of anguish, may find you're extra sensitive to stories and or memories of the past that cause one to cry uncontrollably
- Severe depression that is out of the ordinary
- Severe mood swings
- Sudden apathy for any sentient being or a specific person
- Contagious skepticism and extreme pessimism
- Extreme levels of hatred and resentment
- Sudden feeling as if someone or something (metaphysically) is watching your every move. This most often transpires during sexual intercourse with a partner, when changing clothes, or bathing. (Also known as an intuitive response)

BODY AND ENERGY RESPONSES
- Sudden depletion in energy
- Extremely painful head pains that are not usual. (These would happen only in one part of the head as if someone or

something unseen were stabbing you in the head and or neck.)
- Sudden outbursts of rage wanting to break things and or slam things without logical reason as to why. This would be out of character for the targeted individual.
- One may find they can't stop shaking with fear. This can be accompanied by high levels of anxiety, goosebumps, and cold sweats -especially during and after nightmares.
- Finding burns, bruises and or scratch marks on body that are unexplainable medically and logically to the victim(s).
- Sudden changes in body strength, unable to walk or find pain in certain parts of the body that are unexplainable medically and logically.

These specific descriptions may bring confirmation to you if for any reason you feel your personal space is being invaded either mentally, energetically, or physically.

Entities from the metaphysical realms (the Other Side) have an exceptional impact on the living human psyche that triggers the body to go into a *Warning Mode.* This warning mode is most often *the body reactions one may face which intuitively allows the human to tell when a negative or positive entity is present.* However, it is fair to announce that most humans are not knowledgeable of this due to their consciousness being left in the bliss of unawareness. This text is meant to bring light to that level of consciousness in hopes to sharpen one's awareness. The consciousness is similar to like any other muscle in the body. Only this is a divine intuitive muscle of the soul that most have yet to sharpen, or strengthen through certain levels of spiritual enlightenment. But do not fret, for it is never too late to strengthen this muscle by simply learning how to be more aware of the signs.

Being that you are reading this, it would be fair to suggest you are no longer in the collective and are presently open minded, and or are fully awake from the matrix of illusion. Whether you are reading this for study, help from terror of Demons or familiars, or for future teaching -this is meant to guide, strengthen, and illuminate one to the uncomfortable but brave reality that we are not alone in this incomprehensible universe.

THE DIFFERENCE IN APPEARANCE
THE FREQUENCY EMBODIMENT

Because there are a positive and a negative vibration in the cosmos, there is too the equilibrium of negative and positive entities that coexist within the universe. The energy in souls such as yours is most often filled and fueled by love and compassion thus allowing the soul (energy) embodiment to be that reflection of the feeling and or belief one has in the consciousness. Everything is made up and is constructed by energy and that energy is in exact reflection of what that soulful vibration resides in. There are no exceptions to this due to the Law of Attraction being what we also attract.

When one believes they are worthless, hateful, unloved, undervalued and or unappreciated they will begin to harmonize with that feeling through the energy they are soulfully. This is the same for those that believe they are loving, caring, empathic, selfless, and beautiful -they too shall reflect energetically of that self-belief.

This is to consider the undoubted observation of those that seem to wear the look of sadness within themselves and on their face. A person that is in their twenty's, may in fact be in the physical shape of a thirty or close to forty year old, due to the common stress and perhaps what one continues to focus on internally. This would include negative thoughts and/or beliefs of oneself only to be in the forefront of unfortunate medical and psychological trials.

Same goes for a woman that remains in her strange, yet satisfyingly youthful appearance at fifty-three. For her persistence in positive thoughts and core personal affirmations would serve her well throughout her stages in life. Here it would be sensible to note: energy affects even the most unknowledgeable of persons.

How the energy effects a human being can also have a similar metaphysical effect to an entity's energy frequency. If a departed human spirit, is loving, optimistic with the innate desire to help living humans or animals, then the energetic vibe will be bright, light, and happy to the living. When a departed human spirit is present amongst the living, the response will be a positive impression. As for the negatively charged beings/souls that are ill intended in the spirit realm, the living will begin to experience the equal vibration that negative spirit gives off.

- POSITIVE ENTITY APPARITION EXPERIENCE

    Positive entities are most often reported to be of light beings that are peaceful in a grace that is inexperienced to most humans. These Angel like beings are full of bright light that can seem shiny or similar to a Godlike impression. When loving entities approach a living human their apparition is commonly mentioned as appealing, safe, and bright with affirmation that one can trust intuitively. These spirits of light carry wisdom and knowledge that will speak to you through their energy frequency. It is not every day a living human will be blessed with this experience but is not uncommon enough that it has not been reported to gather significant notice.

- NEGATIVE ENTITY APPARITION EXPERIENCE

    The impact of negative energy, especially by a dark force that is conceived for the purpose of hatred will generate enough fear to cower even the strongest of men and women. These entities most commonly are reported to be of many shapes and sizes due to not having a limitation to what they can portray themselves as. They are shapeless. They are shapeshifters just like Angelic beings allowing their soulful vibration to be what they want in the present moment.

    Some report a dark mist, dark shadow figures that are short like a child or tall like that of a giant. It is apparent that dark entities reside on the opposite side of what is considered good, positive, and or loving. Instead, they are consciously built in their own authentic self, that is embodied by negative emotions, thoughts, and intentions. These are entities that are the absence of light (love).

The impression and experience that is often reported by people over the globe is undeniable when one studies these traits of the supernatural/ Paranormal. The energy vibration of an entity: positive or negative, will also have a sizeable impact on the room that they enter. For example, it is commonly reported by my client's experiences and from those of sharing their own stories that when positive spirits enter a room, or a space, they will feel a very light and positive vibration in that area. They'll report a sense of peace and safety along with a *feeling* as if the room or location were brighter than usual. Even though the light arrangement hasn't changed, they will still catch notice to the lighting impression in the room.

Same goes for those sharing the exact opposite reaction in when a negatively charged spirit enters a vicinity. The person will recall a sense of anxiety, along with invasion of space while acknowledging the *feeling* of lighting being darker than usual. Despite ruling out the possible logical explanations; (electrical wiring malfunctions, dead or dull lightbulbs, etc.) they will go back to recounting everything including the unusual dimness in the location.

As previously mentioned, all spiritual beings carry with them energy vibrations and those vibrations will have an impression carried with them. Just like when a person enters a room, and everyone gravitates to a woman and each person seems to look at her. She may not be very attractive physically even, but her aura (energy field) will *feel* ever positive and uplifting that each person in the room will naturally gravitate towards her due to an intuitive *knowing* she is 'good' to be around. This is due to the person's energy having an impact on the other vibrations in the room causing each person to respond in awareness of this change.

The same goes for the man that enters the same room but comes off to others as 'sketchy' and possibly unsafe to be near. Most would naturally stray from this individual. Even though he may be very handsome and has a nice car, but if he's not very positive emotionally and carries with him much residual negative energy -this will too have the same impact on the crowd -but in the *exact opposite* response.

With this being said, energy of spiritual beings, including humans have massive impressions to the point that those present in the same room will feel this energetic change. Entities, including humans, carry with them energy that could almost be called the *soul's cologne*. Everyone can smell it the instance you walk into the room and can have either a positive impression or a negative one to self and others.

THE ENERGETIC PULL
TRIGGER OBJECTS | DEVICES | RITUALS | PARANORMAL INVESTIGATIONS

The energetic behavior of preternatural & familiar-like entities varies due to having their own level of consciousness, thus allowing the spirit to carry out its own personality. Although the behavioral traits are different
-the cautionary guidelines are *always the same*.

Demonical spirits are attracted to negatively charged behaviors of humans and or spiritual activity that pulls them, encouraging a certain level of spiritual engagement. This energetic pull I speak of is one that enables communication and or direct physical contact with the spirits that which gives the entity free reign in one's life and home. It is through occult devices, dark ritualistic practices, Paranormal investigations, and trigger objects that most often attract the attention of these types of dark entities. Just a simple interest in the Paranormal can attract these malicious entities, however it would depend on the level of interest.

Most often those that attract these types of entities purposely intended this demonical connection, or were not fully aware just how real the supernatural link is between this world and the next by simply looking for answers in their own way. Granted, it is greatly encouraged to seek knowledge in the afterlife, paranormal and the nature of one's sense of existence soulfully/ energetically, but would be *highly* inadvisable to do so through these listed outlets.

Below is a list of the most sought after devices, and techniques in connecting and contacting the dead or other entities. The list is *not* to be limited to only these doorways.

- Ouija Board | Spirit Board | Demon Board (Including homemade) -age of the board is irrelevant
- Séance
- Satanism
- Witchcraft (Black Magic/ conjuring, spell casting)

- Voodoo
- Demon Tarot Cards (store bought or homemade)
- Other conjuring ceremonies
- Black or red candle rituals
- Simply calling out for proof that these entities exist
- Paranormal Investigating (Including EVP: Electronic Voice Phenomenon, Apps that intend to connecting with the dead, etc)
- Through the 'help' of an individual(s) that is doing so without proper guidance/ or full awareness of what they are doing.
- Use of trigger objects (objects that are connected to the dead, or other entities on the Other Side to capture the attention of the spirits.

The use of the devices, ceremonies and or strategies above is not an ideal approach due to the high level of caution that isn't ever mentioned prior. Countless people have come to me in desperation to resolve their rift with an unhappy spirit that they have subsequently summoned during the course of using devices or after preforming conjuring methods. To the extent of pleading for my help over the fact the entities were physically harming them, or their loved ones.

With the use of these types of devices and or ceremonies with the intention to conjure something or someone positive -never guarantees the experience will be. It's a common misconception that if you go into these types of things with only a positive attitude or intention, then you're experience will be in the same -but this couldn't be more *naïve*.

If you look at life, in the same mentality then it will only make sense. Take a neighborhood for example, just because you take a walk in a suburban neighborhood during the day, doesn't mean you won't run into a chance of getting mugged. This is how reality is in both dimensions and should always be treaded carefully with this awareness first, and foremost. Does it mean you should walk in the neighborhood holding your purse close to your chest, or your hand in your pocket grasping your wallet for dear life? No. But it does indicate that as long one has awareness of this being a possibility, it allows you more of a leverage in learning how to prevent it before it happens.

Using a device such as a Ouija board launches what's called a ***portal*** along with a ***psychic signal*** out into the universe to those that are within billions if not trillions of miles away from earth, and other dimensions that are also *within* other dimensions. This transmission goes out into the universe similar to radio waves. These waves of communication travel out into the endless stream of consciousness and galaxies to even lightyears away from earth causing that line of connection to become established. This line of communication occurs so effortlessly that it can happen within a fraction of a second without one being the wiser. Once the signal is transmitted the entities that resonate on that same frequency will hear/feel the transmission loud and clear and will choose to intervene or not through free will.

This psychic signal however doesn't ignite from a device like the Ouija Board, it occurs from the psychic connection that all people have within the universe through the power of thought and desire. The psychic signal happens from *you* and *all* of the other people that participates in the circle of communication. Those that choose to sit in a circle such as during a Ouija Board session or a séance, that circle creates the psychic portal that begins to open the dimension from here to the other side, allowing entities to come and go as they please while leaving you (the participant) as the sitting target for spiritual attack.

Aside from using things like a Ouija Board, entities can be attracted by those that practice the occult such as conducting incantations, practicing black magic such as Witchcraft, Satanism, Voodoo or even Hoodoo. The entities that are most likely to be attracted to these types of practices (including the use of a Ouija board) will be *low vibrational* entities such as human souls that haven't crossed over to the Other Side by choice, or entities like Demons and familiars. Spirits that are low vibrational are in seek of those that are higher in vibration such as the living, and when they become attached to a living person it's most often because the entity is attempting to suck and harness the living person's energy. This is why people become severely depleted in energy such as feeling lack of sleep even after a full 8 hours or more. The entity will be sucking this person's energy throughout the entire night and day due to being a low vibrational spirit. The reason these entities are low in vibration (energy) is due to not ascending past the earth realm and refusing to move forward to the other side. However, sometimes the entity can be a high vibration such as a Demon and have plenty of energy but still suck the human's energy nonetheless causing the human to be so drained that the living person can even start developing severe health complications.

It doesn't take much effort for an entity to find a person that is looking to connect with the Other Side. All it takes is a small amount of curiosity and an open mind for the Spirit to begin to invest into the person's life. Unfortunately, there is a loophole, the entity *doesn't always need verbal consent from the living person to invest into their life.* In fact, all it takes is the person being at the wrong place at the wrong time, such as a person going to a known haunted location to conduct EVP (electronic voice phenomenon) sessions. This person will conduct their experiments, do what they can to catch any credible proof of the Other Side and then go home. However, unknowingly an entity they attracted begins to follow that same person home. Eventually the living person will begin to start noticing things happening that never happened before, which will cause the living person to be suspicious of being legitimately haunted by something intelligent. These entities don't always need a personal invitation, sometimes they will simply follow the living person while they (the living person) unknowingly bring it home because there was something about the person the entity liked and wanted to invest in.

However, the entity can too become attached to the living person(s) by simply moving into a new home, or visiting a new location they haven't been to before, and weren't aware it was haunted. This happens more often than people realize but when it does, it can turn your whole life upside down.

Chapter Two

Identity and Appearance

DEMONS AND FAMILIARS

THE IDENTIFICATION

- **DEMONOLOGY:** *(noun de·mon·ol·o·gy \ dē-mə- 'nä-lə-jē\), (1) the study of demons or evil spirits, (2) belief in demons a doctrine of evil spirits, (3) a catalogue of enemies.*

 -Merriam-Webster English Dictionary, est 1828

One of the most common setbacks when trying to identify a Spirit is when you end up getting information from those that only share what they've read -rather from experience. It's crucial to extract the difference from the type of knowledge one is receiving and how they came about that information. Demonic entities should never be identified into what's more known as a label or a category of sorts. To label someone or something is only putting a set of idolized limitations of the studied entities. These entities or any force one encounters should never be underestimated based on what one were to read, for these energetic beings hold great power to even influence an entire field of men and women to which this causes riots and even wars. It's exceptional to remember that when trying to identify an entity, to remain open to any, and all possibilities of deception, strength, psychic abilities and influence of yourself and others.

In order to understand the entities, one first should be acquired basic knowhow when trying to research from other sources. There's an old saying that no matter what profession you choose to lead, you must occupy yourself with the knowledge of the field through practice. This initiates that no matter how many books you may read, you must also partake in the field through experience to acquire the appropriate kind of wisdom to teach what you've learned. Not everyone is capable of accepting this truth, but it was as true back then, as it is now. However not very many people want to practice through hard work, patience, and learning from those that have already traveled through the same path.

ACQUIRED KNOWLEDGE: *The study of the field that which one wishes to partake. Referring to sources for the experience and acquired knowledge of others.*

FIELD KNOWLEDGE: *The art of acquiring wisdom through the act of participating through that which you have studied and heard.*

It doesn't matter how many books one reads or how many stories one hears, if one has not experienced the material they are writing, instructing, or influencing -than they are no more knowledgeable than an elementary school teacher attempting brain surgery.

To elaborate, these sorts of energies don't identify themselves to a limited concept such as a spiritual practice or religious belief. No matter the level of faith one has, these diabolical entities don't suppose one's will based on faith (belief in a higher power), but on inner belief of one's worth, self-love and conscious desire of existence.

However, do they have an individual identity with set abilities? -YES. It is most commonly believed by those of a religious belief that malevolent beings are only to be identified as 'damned' souls that were condemned by a higher power, like God. *This is not the case.* The harsh reality from my in-depth experience with these multi-dimensional beings is they are not limited to the spirituality of humanity. Instead they are only driven and motivated by the energy and emotion of *fear.*

THE TRUE IDENTITY
APPEARANCE AND CHARACTERISTICS

WARNING

As an advanced and thoroughly trained Psychic Medium, and Demonologist that has traveled through dimensions (not only including the Astral Realm) -I've been targeted by physical and psychic attacks by these malicious monsters for the threat of this book is vital. As hard to believe as this may seem, my very life has been at stake to write this book. But my passion to help guide you back to the Source is far greater of importance. The imagery, information and knowhow that is presented in this guide, is something no other Psychic or Demonologist has demonstrated nor acknowledged. Respectfully, as eloquently helpful the fellow interpretations have been, this piece of knowledge you'll be proceeding toward is information these entities don't want you to know and has never been expressed for it requires exceptional tolerance and experience. This isn't based on what I've read or heard, this is based on fact through unfortunate Psychic Medium experiences and countless client testimonies.

As you proceed, do so with
CAUTION!!!

In order to know your opponent -one must know it's authenticity. It's like that old saying, *Keep your friends close, but keep your enemies closer.* This saying suggests that, in order to remain one step ahead as much as humanly possible, -one must remain aware of the capabilities of your enemy at all times. Keeping a watchful eye on them but through trained awareness -not obsession. Remaining readily aware of this difference is *cautiously advised.*

True authenticity doesn't just appear based on words, but through actions and through signs of intentions or agenda. The side of this earthly world is not as foreign to the metaphysical world, for these dark beings have been roaming the earth plane for thousands of years. However, it wasn't until recently in the past few decades were these forces being 'called out' and quickly responded to.

The human mind can only comprehend and take so much information at a time, and these entities are highly aware of this due to their advanced abilities and centuries of practice with close observation of the human race. Although they are aware of what we may be able to handle -they also know what we cannot, and this is where their approach comes into play.

Demonical entities and are not limited to how they will appear to us. Anyone that tries to tell you in books, or in other forms of teaching this are highly naïve to the limitless potential and motivation of these spirits. Demons, including familiar beings will approach their target based on what frightens them the most. The spirit will intercept into your deepest and most precious of memories, along with worst nightmares, or fears to give them a gateway toward incomprehensible intimidation and terror. Terror, is not a word I use lightly. What they are capable of pursuing are enriched maneuvers to conquer your quest for self-love, and personal exploration of the higher self. Once these spirits have that key of your worst fears, they will appear to you with this rooted key in mind.

Here is a brief list of some of the ways Demons and Familiars may appear to you either as an apparition on the earth realm or in dream state (where you can be placed into other Realms -this will be discussed later).

DEMONSTRATIVE FORMS OF APPEARANCE

- Dark shadow figure (so dark that it seems solid).
- Dark shadow fog or mist.
- As Jesus Christ or another advanced Deity *(They are tricksters)*
- Dark shadowy dog or some other kind of animal.
- As a departed loved one (will be heavily discussed further)
- As a being or person that is exceptionally sexual and even *forcibly* seductive (will be heavily discussed further)
- An entity of a dark appearance with glowing red eyes.
- An entity that appears maliciously gruesome with horns and a tail (very rare) and with sharp claws.
- As a little girl or boy, asking for help saying, 'he' or 'she' is lost, or asking to play.

- Appear in the middle of the night with seemingly gruesome features that you'd only see in movies, or read in horror stories. (These entities crave fright)

The brief appearances are not to be limited to only this. Again, I repeat,
-they are **NOT TO BE LIMITED** to only what is listed as the expected appearances for these beings are highly advanced powerful creatures with *no mercy for humanity*.

Have you ever heard the phrase, "Don't judge a book by it's cover."? This is true beyond words. The phrase alone indicates the importance to not take the face for it's authenticity. To not take what you see for granted by underestimating the appearance as the only honest approach. This is as true here on the earth realm as it is on the other side. The difference however is the skills to discern the difference.

Before we continue, I want to discuss the word, ***Discernment*** -what do you think it means? The common religious belief is that discernment is a 'gift' from the 'holy spirit' -however this is a *false interpretation*. Discernment means to have the ability to decipher the difference between one thing and another. In order to *know* what is and what isn't. The 'gift' of discernment isn't a 'gift' from a higher power, but the *gift of one's awareness*. In other words, it is the ability one acquires through sheer will to awaken the knowhow from within with the gift of ***intuition***. It is Intuition that is a gift all possess that is meant to be honed and accelerated for this very purpose

-to access truth from untruth.

This is part of the knowledge that the Demons and Familiars don't want you to acquire. For once you've learned and accepted this, you will gain your power back through faith in one's ability of further self-discovery.

Now that you're aware of what your intuition's purpose is meant for, now it's time to learn the steps in using this gift of discernment.

To add, I also like to call intuition, your **Divine Message Receiver** for the information you're receiving is through the energy vibrations of the person, situation, or spirit that you're encountering or about to encounter. When one has a negative *gut feeling,* this feeling is sending an energetic signal to your body to allow you the clues to what's about to occur as a gentle warning in advanced. However, it is still through our Free Will where we can choose to accept and heed this warning or not. It is through experience that one will feel they should have listened to their gut feeling, but don't let this discourage your confidence. This is merely an opportunity given to us from the Source of ourselves by listening to our intuition that is a part of all of us. There is no 'right' or 'wrong' by placing fault on the individual when it comes to following intuition, for this is also based on a developed trust of your own levels of *knowing* that cannot be *known and understood* without first experiencing.

How Demons and other negatively charged entities will appear is based on an individual aspect of what is considered scary to the person they are haunting. For example, if a person is frightened by insects, then the Demon will intercept into your consciousness a nightmare of you being eaten and consumed by insects. No person's level of what is considered scary will be the same as the next person, which is why understanding their target is crucial when undergoing their appearance.

Discerning an entity based on it's physical appearance can be challenging at best if you aren't taught the hints and tips to tell what type of energy they are and their intentions. Most often people are under the misunderstanding through the Christian belief that if you are approached by an attractive appearing spirit like a male energy, that it must be Lucifer in disguise. This is a *myth*. Reason being is because if this were always the case, then you would never be able to trust even the most benevolent beings that approach you either on the earth realm, or in your dream state for they are too attractive, beautiful beings of light. This would only cause confusion and lack of trust of your own senses through your Divine Message Receiver. Instead, what I like to teach my clients that seek my Paranormal Advisory, is to pay close attention to not just their appearance but also their *words* and how they make you *feel* internally in your energy.

Don't get me wrong, there are many deceiving entities that will attempt to lure you with physical attraction, but they will also bait you with flattery, through power, greed, ego, and through sexual promiscuity. However, let this not be confused with love making through the emotion of passionate desire. Passion is an emotion expressed through the act of giving but sexual promiscuity is an emotion that is expressed through the act of taking with control and greed. There is a fine difference between the two.

There are entities such as Demons that hold the ability to transform into someone you could trust at first glance, such as a departed loved one that you've longed to see again. The entity will lure you by falsifying their appearance in hopes to gain your trust by looking like your loved one. However, even the most advanced Demons and Familiars aren't going to hold up this cloak for very long. Even the most skilled of entities will carry a flaw or two of their false appearance.

I know this for during my time as a professional Psychic Medium I've been approached by these *very* experiences. They would approach me like my departed loved one, but within a matter of seconds I could tell it wasn't my loved one for their appearance began to show signs of inconsistent characteristics that weren't similar to my loved one.

With the tips I'm about to share you'll be able to recognize these signs of inconsistencies that will not only help you, but may astound you with alarming validation if you've had these encounters before. But I implore you to not place blame on yourself, this happens to even the most exceptionally trained prophets and spiritual teachers, *no one is immune to these encounters.*

Below is a list of characteristic traits, and physical alterations that may alert your awareness to the truth of the happening. You can use this list of tips to also discern the difference in dream state and other realms such as the Astral Realm.

QUESTIONABLE PHYSICAL APPEARANCES

- The entity will be paler than usual, like missing a natural appearing skin pigment. Almost as if they are dead.
- The entity may also have a smell about them that seems rotten, or unpleasant to the senses.
- The entity's eyes will begin to alter and change, or may not be the same color as your original memory of your departed loved one.
- The entity may smile in a way that seems creepy. Almost as if they smile with a secret agenda in mind but won't tell you what it is.
- The entity may smile, but their teeth are sharp, or may even be missing, rotten or broken.
- Spirits that appear may be bright and luminous, but then after a few minutes this will change and seem darker and unfriendly. This may become extremely uncomfortable.
- The spirit may appear with bruising, scars, burns or scratch marks that are either small, or large.
- The encountered entity may appear as someone you can trust, but then change it's form, or body part that can be odd or questionable.
- The Spirit may speak to you with ease, but then when you're next to them they seem to have bad breath.
- The entity approaching you may say they are an Angel but appear to you as a dark entity with red or black eyes.

Although this is a descriptive list, keep in mind that these are only a select few examples of how they may appear and then change, leaving you in fair amount of doubt of their authenticity. Spirits are driven by their energy frequency as stated earlier. However most often people can be so focused on what the Spirit says rather than also taking time to consider their appearance and or even the environment that the Spirit took you to in dream state.

It is not only the appearance of the entity that one must take into account, but of the characteristics and what the entity says and or does. In order to discern the Spirit thoroughly, one should take into all angles of the levels of engagement when being approached. This here, is where many would say is the part where you *'test the Spirit'* -which is true to *an extent.* However, it is advised to not test the Spirit based on only a religious view point, but based on the intentions of the entity. Demons and familiar Spirits know the Bible *extremely* well, but they are not threatened by said scripture, but by the course of the will and faith of the individual through courage and love.

To test a Spirit's authenticity, it's highly advisable to remain calm, and to NEVER challenge the entity. For if you do, you will be sadly mistaken on their ability to cause great regret later. Their abilities are not without full function of grasping your very soul and briefing the consciousness with fright so unbearable, that it may cause one to go literally insane, and or to take one's own life. I say this *heavily.* Countless clients have begged for my help from all over the world due to challenging the Demon's that were haunting them, that they were left with nothing but to cling to their own sanity before seeing the light again, after much cleansing, and clearing of these negative vibrations and Spirits.

When testing a Spirit, I recommend relying heavily upon one's intuition more so than just on religion or another belief system. For your intuition will grant you an advantage that when the Spirit speaks a lie -you'll be able to discern this without struggle. The way to hone your intuition is based on trusting your initial feeling you have that comes into your consciousness the moment something is said, done, or happening. Focus on your initial feelings by asking yourself, *"Does this feel good or bad?"* If you were to answer this question with an immediate, "this feels bad." -then this is the moment you'll know that this spirit cannot be trusted.

After countless client interviews and testimonies of those that asked for my counsel, along with experiences of my own, I've been able to sum up a brief, yet detailed list of what these next few hints are when discerning unfriendly entities. I bring caution however, for some of this information may be unsettling to some readers.

QUESTIONABLE CHARACTERISTICS

- The entity may start speaking to you in a harsh tone that brings only discomfort and fear to your energy.
- The entity may begin to speak loudly, or aggressively as if in assertion to control or belittle you.

- The entity may begin to talk oddly, such as speaking words backwards -this would be as if you're taking a record player and playing the record in reverse.
  - The entity may begin to speak causing you to shutter. This is caused by the negative intention to intimidate, and cause alarm and fear. *This is what they want* in your response.
  - The entity that you're approached by may seem friendly and loving at first, but then quickly begin to call you names, or bring things up from your past to encourage guilt, shame, or sadness.
  - The entity may seem alluring at first by being seductive or charming, but then may quickly become abrasive or forceful. An example could be where the entity may attempt to rape, or sexually assault you or someone else. This is not to be taken lightly, for the version of this metaphysical experience can be *excruciatingly painful and traumatizing*. This is exceptionally common from sexual Demons such as an **Incubus** or a **Succubus.**
  - The entity may encourage you to preform sexual acts that you are not comfortable with. They may even use force with a sickening pleasure through your intimidation and fear.
  - The entity's level of perversion may appear to you in a sense that would alarm you. It may begin to do sexual acts, or other certain behaviors that you wouldn't have prepared for.
  - When being approached by a negatively charged entity, it will ask you to do things, but if you're answer is "No", and it still encourages without care to how you feel -this is a definite warning. You're departed loved ones, or any benevolent beings won't push you to do something you

aren't comfortable doing. They may ask, but if you decline, they will respect this. Malevolent beings won't care!
- During your encounter, if you experience a moment where the entity begins to twitch or stutter that isn't the usual behavior of your departed loved one, take heed to this.
- If you encounter a Spirit that begins to start speaking in a rough tone of voice that makes your energy tremble with fear and caution -then it's advisable to listen to your instinct.
- If the entity you encounter begins to start hitting you, or harming you in any way physically, psychicly, or emotionally on purpose, then this is not your loved one nor a benevolent Spirit.

After taking time to read through these bullets, I hope this guides you to another level of understanding of how intelligently clever and ruthless these beings can be when given the opportunity. It's a tragedy to the human race, for there is no age limit to these being's agenda. They will terrorize even the most innocent of humanity such as infants, children, to even those that are mentally unstable or incapable of defending themselves.

Chapter Three

Advanced Abilities

THEIR COSMIC POWER

What most are usually unaware of is the potential of the capabilities of these ferocious figures. The abilities these entities possess is not to be underestimated, for the very mention of them in a dare to express this with little respect, will only lead you down the darkened rabbit hole of misery and deep regret. Their levels of attacks are cunning, sharp, and extremely strategic and if for any reason they aren't successful in their original plan, they will stop at nothing to do what they must to reach their goal: which is to make you believe that fear is more powerful than you.

As we continue there will be tactics I will share to engage you in a deeper concept of the Demonic mindset -but remain weary of your own level of intentions. This is exceptionally crucial for the moment you become hooked in the idea of what most would call, *fascination*, you'll uncover something degrading and dissatisfying.

PSYCHIC ABILITIES

People that undergo Demonical hauntings or from a Familiar Spirit may experience what's commonly called, **Psychic Attacks.** These attacks may appear subtle at first, but can rapidly turn into your worst nightmare even during the daytime. Psychicly, these entities hold the abilities to know everything there is to know about you. However, many are under this closed belief that Demons don't have such abilities, that only God does, or Jesus Christ. However, this is again, another viral myth that needs to be addressed. These beings are not limited, so in truth they are in fact extremely versatile in addressing the core of your very emotions that will either implant hope, or unceasing doom within your very soul.

I know this because I've experienced this terrifying turmoil for years after exploring and studying the Demonology field. As a person that believes that you never really know something until you've experienced it yourself, can you truly comprehend and demonstrate the authenticity of the findings and facts. Although I was willing, I've quickly uncovered a world that was unbeknownst to not just me, but to most of the population on this planet. And even though those that are haunted by these beings didn't ask for this, I still had to uncover the truth as to *why* they were still being targeted.

During my time assisting clients and even families, I would begin to receive *blows* from out of the blue, in my head, not knowing exactly where they came from. These blows would feel as if someone took a knife and literally stabbed my brain. It would be so painful in just one spot of my head that I'd bend over in pain wondering where it came from. Alongside, I'd begin to endure incomprehensible night terrors that were so gruesome and daunting, they'd cause me to awaken screaming in a cold sweat that soaked from head to toe. These forces are not playing around. To anyone that is ever considering being a Demonologist, or to even read this book, you're already being closely watched and observed, for your very *existence* of interest can be a *threat*. And to who is considered a potential threat of their goal to overtake the human race, they will stop at nothing to get what they want.

The list of potential psychic attacks are numerous, below are a few that are known to be exceptionally common. These attacks are not only for the "psychic" folk (Psychic Mediums, Mystics, etc.), for all people possess the psychic ability -but only a seldom few hone this skill toward self-mastery.

- **Extreme Night Terrors.** These nightmares are beyond the occasional bad dream. These types are extremely graphic, with a level of lucidity where you'll be able to recall smells, tastes, feelings, conversations, or other sensations along with remembering the sounds of things occurring. You'll experience a series of these that seem almost endless to the point where you'll be fearful to sleep again.

- **Massive Head Pains or Stabs.** These types of pains will occur on one part of the head. Most often people describe an excessive stabbing sensation to the brain or back of the neck. It will be different from a headache, for a headache is like an uncomfortable ringing of the brain. Psychic head injuries will be as if someone took a massive blow to your skull.

- **Uncensored Memories or Images.** Here you may experience moments where you're suddenly getting terrible visions of you harming someone you love. This will be completely out of the ordinary of your mindful behavior. Some will testify to have images float into their mind of murdering their children, spouse, or pet without any reasonable or logical cause. (*If this were to happen, don't feel shame for this is what the entities want you to feel*). Memories that are uncomfortable to you may arise unexpectedly. More often these memories will seem so surreal as if you're reliving it all over again.

- **Excessive Draining of Energy.** You may find you had a full eight hours of night's sleep only to discover you're more tired than you were the night before. This is because of the Spirit draining your energy similar to that of a vampire. By doing so, the entity will position itself next, on top, or underneath you during sleep, and begin to suck your energy from your vibration. This will be a considerable amount that it leaves the human body low in restfulness. (Vampires don't exist -just FYI).

- **Astral Realm Attacks.** This is for those that find themselves suddenly in what's called ***Astral Projection.*** This is where the victim is most likely going to experience an out-of-body experience during sleep state. During this experience victims will recall an invisible force pulling their soul out of their body during sleep mode, and then begin doing things to them. This is unsettling because the living person being attacked may not know how to get out of this, and will find they are alone with this entity. The series of these types of Astral attacks can be similar to physical harm on the earth realm. Hits, being thrown around in your room, experiencing rape or other levels of sexual assault. The entity will not always be invisible but can be if chooses.

- **Sleep Paralysis.** *Sleep Paralysis* will be explained in several different ways by many other sources. But what I have concluded as a Psychic Medium with an advanced ability to see beyond this physical realm is that when you experience this, it's due to a lower vibrational entity. Sleep Paralysis will be when you awaken from sleep but find your body is immobile and cannot seem to move your neck, legs, or any part of your body. Your consciousness will be fully functioning, and you'll ask yourself why this may be happening to you, but this is not because your body is relapsing, or failing. This is due to an entity putting your body into a paralysis state causing you to become immobile, so they can harness your energy further. This is considerably unsettling to some that experience this. But don't be too alarmed, you can surpass this after a conscious effort to awaken your muscles again. During Sleep Paralysis, you may also find you can see out of your **Third Eye**. This is where your body is completely asleep, but you seem to see out of your *center eye* that is just above the center of the eye brows. You may even hear another person in your home or environment, or something that is lurking among you. This is because your psychic abilities have awakened and the entity that is causing your Sleep Paralysis is aware of your awakened abilities to take notice of them. Most likely the entity will still attempt to remain invisible to not let you see them. But if you were to see while using your third eye, it can be exceptionally uncomfortable, and even scary for you're unable to move away from the entity that is invading your space.

It isn't unusual to undergo these types of experiences during a psychic attack by a negative spirit such as a Demon or a Familiar, for their powers are greatly advanced. What is unusual however, is if one were to be presented with the attacks, but not *also* suffer from severe bad luck.

Bad luck is another form of a psychic attack due to the entities wishing nothing but bad energy upon you while they are bringing the targeted individual continual streams of uneasy situations. This case of bad luck will come in a series of situations that seem to happen one right after the other. It will be severely unusual to even the most unlikely of those that may never appear to have bad luck of any kind. Bad luck and **Good luck** do exist. What it is, is another story. Luck, from my recent experiences and in-depth understanding of the cosmos is a stream of either *positive wishful energy or negative wishful energy.* This is based on the consciousness (soul) of either the living or the departed composing their psychic energy to construct a positive experience or a negative experience. This is similar to how prayer occurs. An answered prayer, is simply collective positive psychic energy occurring within the course of the Universe that which allows the wishful streams of events to occur.

The types of Bad Luck will be a construct of collaborated and measured disadvantages as a series of events. The kinds of bad luck one may encounter during a psychic attack is listed below -but are not meant to be limited to only what is listed for the potential is limitless!

- You're late for work but your car won't start.
- You set your alarm for work but then find that your alarm never went off at the time it was set.
- The power to your home has suddenly shut off for no apparent reason.
- You or a close loved one has recently been in a car accident.
- You may experience a major appliance in your home has stopped working, broke or even exploded without warning.
- You may experience a flood due to bad weather, or due to plumbing in the home that went terribly wrong.
- May experience slipping on water, or tripping in your home. May experience falling down the stairs without reasonable cause.

- Your hair may begin to fall out more so, but you don't find reasonable cause to this. *(it's advisable to speak to your local doctor first before relying completely on a spiritual explanation.)*
- You may find that your cash in your purse or wallet has gone missing without an explanation.
- You may find that suddenly your credit card is overdrawn due to someone stealing your card information.
- You suddenly discover you or your family has an outbreak of lice.
- Experiences a series of earthquakes that appear to be more common than usual.

There are countless of ways one will encounter what's considered Bad Luck, but it is highly recommended to not allow these types of unfortunate events to get the better of you. Allow your emotions to process the situation for a fair amount of time. Express your grief if you must do so, but don't dwell on it, for this level of unhappy emotions will only feed the negatively charged entities more. This is why they bring these unfortunate events, so they can get you to where they want you psychologically and emotionally. Don't let them win!

TELEPATHY

For the entity to see more into your inner dialog they use a Psychic ability known as **Telepathy.** This is *the ability to communicate from one mind to another using extrasensory means of the consciousness. A transferring of one mind's thought waves to another.* However, this is not a means to learn more about you energetically but intellectually. This particular strategy is where the entity will attempt to psychicly communicate with you within your mind where you may find yourself hearing a voice that isn't familiar to your own. It will begin to speak to you saying things about you, or encourage unhealthy or harmful behavior that is out of your character. Here, is the place where the targeted individual may start to question his or her own sanity. The entity is enticed when doubt creeps into the human target for they are then at an advantage to perpetrate that very point to allow them a greater chance at success.

It is not unusual to begin to take notice of this when one were to experience dreams or Paranormal activity in the home, or work place. Most often the person that is being targeted will acknowledge the voice speaking to them during a nightmare, or during a moment they swear they saw a dark shadowy figured in their home. This is because the malevolent figure is attempting open communication by intercepting their level of thought to your level of thought through the manipulation of energy frequency.

There is only one form of telepathic communication, by sending thought waves to another level of consciousness. With this, fairly concludes that Demonic and Familiar entities not only possess a soul (consciousness), but are fully capable of manipulating your own thoughts to a distortion so vial that it can leave the victim discombobulated intellectually. The way the thoughts will intercept into your mind will appear as like a random thought, image, or feeling. When this occurs, one must take a moment to assess their own findings and digest the culprit before them in this moment.

As a Psychic Medium I've encountered several interfering thought waves that were not my own. In moments of confusion I would ask myself if this were my thought, or someone else's. The best way to discern the difference is to listen to one's intuition and take the first initial thought (answer) that enters your mind -that will also be guided by your emotions through a 'gut feeling'.

There were moments in dream state where I was faced with an uncensored imagery of a terrible sort, so horrific it's close to impossible to justly describe. The entity of what could be best described as an abomination to existence itself -began to speak to me within my mind with the ability of Telepathy. Here the entity would have a full conversation with me without it's mouth needed to be used. After much needed practice over the course of my time as a Psychic, I've learned to master this same ability. However, the memory of this experience will haunt me for the rest of my life for the very words expressed from this being only exposed fear and pure evil.

Telepathy is not usual to those that haven't awakened from the illusions of this physical world. In turn, it is gravely popular that those who share these said experiences, thus are accused of being mentally unstable. Those that are put into psychiatric hospitals, or treatment centers are most often mistaken as being 'crazy', when in truth, they are in the dealings of facing this demonical attack alone feeling shame and guilt. Demonical taunts aren't to solely suggest that all individuals identified to their own personified irregular mental compacity is the singular cause. But to promote the probability of the threat itself with an open mind.

PSYCHOKINESIS

One of the more advanced Psychic abilities is the power of **Psychokinesis**, which is *the production of motion in objects without contact or other physical means.* The ability to levitate objects (large or small), people and even animals. This is exceptionally dangerous for the victims of this type of ability may suffer several types of experiences. Below is a list of a few examples when Psychokinesis is used:

- Objects being thrown across a room.
- Objects being levitated in mid-air.
- Finding an object large, or small was thrown at you, or another person.
- A person, animal, or a group of people are levitated or tossed across a room.

This particular ability is one of the more threatening due to the suppressed potential to the harm that can be done to the victim, or the entire family that is being **Oppressed** during the second stage of a Demonical haunting, *(will discuss further in later part.)* Those that are mentally traumatized by this terrifying experience can and do tend to forever suffer from severe PTSD (Post Traumatic Stress Disorder) symptoms along with triggers. The magnitude can excel to a level beyond human comprehension and even from a respected science explanation.

Psychokinesis requires an immense amount of focus from the consciousness that is preforming the motions of the objects or people. This is where the conscious entity will intently imagine with their psychic ability to maneuver one item to another location. The ability is similar to any other muscle of the human body, the only difference however is the muscle is the power of the mind. Although human souls are too capable of this ability, it is rare for a human to actually be successful. This ability in simplicity, is the function of the energetic muscles of the mind to move physical objects, or people as one pleases. In turn, requires great amounts of core belief of one's capability - thus explains the magnitude of destruction if done so by a force beyond this world.

MATERIALIZATION

Dematerialization and **Rematerialization** are a specialty when it comes to a progressive malevolent figure, for it's the craft of manipulating physical objects. This is where the entity will maintain impressive focus on the object of their choosing, and dissect the object's matter to the point where they're energetically granted the agility of making it disappear and reappear. This is similar to teleportation of the object and causing it to leave this realm for a temporary time, then when they choose, they will manifest it again but perhaps in a different spot. Sometimes the object will be dematerialized and may never reappear at all, causing the Oppressed living human to question where their object went.

Here it's a considerable opportunity and intention to orchestrate the moments this happens to lead the person to wonder their logic and memory. Those that have experienced this would express they'd have a specific item in need, but then somehow always seemed to 'misplace it', and unable be able to recover it. Not sure if this were simply accidental, the person would go buy the same item to replace the missing one. But within less than forty-eight hours that same item would go 'missing' -yet again. This is incredibly common and is not the person losing sense of their sanity, but being tricked into believing and fearing this is so.

The purpose of this is simple, *to cause one to go into a state of internal panic of one's sanity.* If one were to begin to be convinced they can't even commit to the placement of a simple object, then who's to say they won't also lose sight of themselves or of those they love. This is increasingly tactful and crude but it's what they do in order to put you right where they want you -*doubtful of your own sanity.*

AN IMMEASURABLE THREAT

Demons and other negatively charged forces are not bound by the concept of time like earth time. Instead they are free from such limitations allowing them the ultimate advantage. This is gravely discouraging for the possibilities of probable attacks and strategic manipulative setups are greatly increased. These beings are multi-dimensional entities that are boundless by time with a ravaging thirst for sabotage.

Just like Angels, and other Ascended beings, they are able to be at more than one place at a time without stress. It is in the Demons habitual cosmic nature to desire the very thing you fear, and to bring that fear to life. Due to their insatiable ability to travel between multiple dimensions simultaneously, they are capable of terrorizing you and another person across the world at the *same time.*

This is something most Demonologists don't share because of not being fully aware of just how limitless these beings are themselves. Demons and other Familiars can insert themselves in your dream state giving you the worse nightmare, while also doing the same thing to the rest of your family simultaneously, at the same exact time. Then when you all wake up, you'll share how you had a terrible nightmare, then to no surprise they too may share they had the same, or similar experience. This is not unusual and is to be fully expressed with haste for this is happening to people every day all over the world, and are left with nothing left but to pray for a miracle. However, this guide you are holding now, will hopefully present to you that said opportunity to grant you an upper hand on how to handle and evade these types of diabolical creatures.

Chapter Four
Cosmic Origin vs Religion

UNLEARN TO LEARN

It is a widely spread tradition to instruct from a rooted belief amongst Christianity that Demons and Familiars are a threat to mankind by the wrath sent from the Devil, Satan or commonly known as Lucifer. Among the Christian faith is the insatiable accusation of those that disbelieve in the word of the Holy Bible's scriptures, that one must be under instruction or guidance, or even being Possessed by the Devil himself. As old fashioned as this may seem, it's still a deeply unsettling practice by many Bible followers to this day. I can attest to this for I receive countless letters from those of this 'faith' accusing me of being a Satan worshipper, a Witch, a "Demon whore", -even to the extent that I sold my soul to the Devil.

It is no surprise from human's research throughout history that the Christian teachers were ruthless, merciless of free thinking to make one's own choices in a spiritual practice that didn't agree with their own. They're motivation over a thousand years ago hasn't changed, for the fear driven concept, to run to a higher power through a closed belief system, will somehow save one from the Demonic wrath of evil remains as it's instructed teachings. And although as well intended as these rules and regulations were thought to be, it's no shock for one to conclude the power and influence from the church was nearly boundless in it's capabilities to motivate the town's people through fear in history.

I'm sure you've heard the phrase: *History repeats itself.?* Here is to emphasis the word, *repeat* due to the undeniable reality that most would simply turn the other cheek. Truth be told, as uncomfortable this next piece may be, it would be a shame if I didn't tell you the *God* honest truth. I'm a realist. I call things for what they are, regardless for the judgments or the backlash, but I'm also a kind hearted being that believes whole heartedly the power of love and guidance is what prevails us as a people. But -it remains to be, that it is *truth* that guides one out of misery. But this truth will require a courage to remain aware of one's stance within the making of your own journey. This book isn't just meant as a guide of Demonology, but to also guide you to the core essence of one's I AM (consciousness). However, in order to embrace truth, we must first unlearn what we've been taught for centuries.

THE BIBLE

There are well over fifty different books of the Bible, each with it's own version of spiritual emphasis, composition and even doctrinal angles. With this finding of fact alone, should cause one to be fumbled as to *why* such a holy sanctioned 'word' must be rewritten so many times. Take a moment to ponder this as you proceed...

The Bible isn't honored as the ultimate source of spiritual salvation for those in just the United States, but has been a vital guide for Islamic culture as well. The 'Word of God', is being exhausted for the world is now taking a rough look in the context, that which was reworded for centuries. Questioning now it's authority from the not only crude narrative, but through it's many continuous contradictions. Bible scholars along with historians most often tend to find agreement that many of the stories in the Bible face questionable doubt when being compared to the Ten Commandments. Though the Ten Commandments are meant as the spoken and written rules declared as the regulations of God, the people and intentions of the stories never cease to surprise even the most educated.

The 'Good Book' is really a variety of books that were written by human authors which has been the conclusion to scholars and religious experts. However, despite their impressive research, there remains to be those that find the Bible being the only source of words written by God
-*literally*.

In fairness, the Bible holds some levels of moral ground, such as loving your neighbor, not committing adultery, thievery, or to murder another sentient being. However even these targeted subjects that are held as some of the Ten Commandments, have been known throughout the Old and New Testament to lose credibility as a positive notion due to the lengths of the stories and their end results. Some of the stories in the Bible are so dark it cannot help but leave even the harshest level for imagination to become utterly disturbed. Yet, the Gospels, and widely spoken and worshipped prophets such as Moses are taught throughout history and nations that were of good nature. When in truth, most are not aware that Moses was in fact a mass murderer and rapist while killing thousands of innocent women and children in cold blood. It was Moses who urged his troops to *'kill every male among the little ones, and kill every woman that hath known man by lying with him.'* The virgin girls, however, were to be *spared*, and brought back as prisoners. It was 32,000 that were taken after this occurred and brought back to their home. This wasn't a moment of saving lives like many portray -this was a *massacre* along with human trafficking being done.

Discoveries such as this I personally could never find true comfort, yet somehow the modern Christian creates a dialog attempting to rationalize with some sort of a moral compass of the Gospels even after being aware of the reveal. This is what troubles me, and not as a Psychic Medium, but as a temporary human being on the earth. Concerned for the human consciousness' capability to discern mythical fantasy from the harsh realities of truth. Though -not solely should one be compared to another's level of awareness when it comes to discerning myth from fact, for it is carefully based on one's experience through the individual's *awakening* process that all undergo in their own time.

In order to fully comprehend the true authority within this 'sacred' book, one must take a moment to carefully evaluate all that lies within it. Here are a few of the scriptures that I've taken a liberty to add for your spiritual enlightenment. The words of 'God' that one is socially ordered to follow with good intent and obedience for one's salvation, consists of and are in support of **rape, incest, murder, sacrifice (human and animal), slavery,** and other levels of human indecency.

There's no trickery here, nothing is worded unjustly -these are actual scriptures in the Bible. Due to the recent said differences, it is expected to find each scripture may be interpreted slightly different, but sternly put -the *intentions* through the messages are *still the same.*

GENESIS 19:34
"And it came to pass on the morrow, that the firstborn said unto the younger, Behold, I lay yesternight with my father: let us make him drink wine this night also; and go thou in, and lie with him, that we may preserve seed of our father."
KING JAMES VERSION (KJV)

ISAIAH 13:16
"Their children also shall be dashed to pieces before their eyes; their houses shall be spoiled, and their wives ravished."
KING JAMES VERSION (KJV)

FOOT NOTE: The word, 'Ravished' was meant to describe the act of rape back in those days.

HOSEA 13:16
"The people of Smaria must bear their guilt, because they have rebelled against their God. They will fall by the sword; their little ones will be dashed to the ground, their pregnant women ripped open."
NEW INTERNATIONAL VERSION (NIV)

EXODUS 21:20-21
"Anyone who beats their male or female slave with a rod must be punished if the slave dies as a direct result, but they are not to be punished if the slave recovers after a day or two, since the slave is their property."
NEW INTERNATIONAL VERSION (NIV)

NUMBERS 31:17-18
"Now kill all the boys. And kill every woman who has slept with a man, but save for yourself every girl who has never slept with a man."
NEW INTERNATIONAL VERSION (NIV)

SAMUEL 15:3
"Now go and smite Amalek, and utterly destroy all that they have, and spare them not; but slay both man and woman, infant and suckling, ox and sheep, camel and ass."
KING JAMES VERSION (KJV)

'THOU SHALT NOT KILL,' said the Commandment, -but even the God in the Bible is known to ordering even the adorned prophets to commit terrible atrocities in the name of the Lord. Sounds more like to me this particular 'God', was and still remains to be a downright hypocrite.

There are countless scriptures where the Bible's God orders obedient and devoted servants to kill children, men and women in the name of the Lord, and by doing so the person would be found pleasing to the Lord. Not to mention the many wars in the stories were not so justified -for the reasons behind most of the wars within the Gospels were of revenge, greed and of false entitlement.

In fact, it is not considered taboo for God in the Bible to test one's loyalty by temptation of murdering your child through a sacrificial ceremony with burnt offering. For in the book of Isaac, Abraham, was forced to accept that he was to lose his second son, Isaac -by his own hand, for 'God did tempt him' through a test of loyalty.

> *"And he said, take now thy son, thine only son Isaac, whom thou lovest, and get thee into the land of Moriah; and offer him there for a burnt offering upon one of the mountains which I will tell thee of." (22,1)*

Abraham did what God instructed him to, even though he was reluctant to do so -still wanted to find salvation in the Lord through obedience. He took his young men and son with him and clave the wood for the burnt offering, then went to the place where God told him to be. Once Abraham reaches his destination, he tells his helpers to wait while he takes the wood, to ready the fire, then leads Isaac to the alter and lays him upon it -knife in ready.

> *"And Abraham stretched forth his hand, and took the knife to slay his son. And the angel of the Lord called onto him out of heaven, and said, Abraham, Abraham: and he said, Here am I. And he said, Lay not thine hand upon the lad, neither do thou any thing unto him: for now I know that thou fearest God, seeing thou hast not withheld thy son, thine only son from me.*

And Abraham lifted up his eyes, and looked, and behold behind him a ram caught in a thicket by his horns: and Abraham went and took the ram, and offered him up for a burnt offering in the stead of his son." (22,14).

Arguably those seeking to disarm the discomforts of this scripture go extra lengths in relying on some kind of a underlying logic behind this inexcusable trip to 'loyalty'. But all the same, no parent in their right mind would say this is the way to test another person's ability to hold loyalty -but a treason of sorts through one's logic and rationality. Why would a loving source of authority deem it ever necessary to hold one's kin to the tip of a knife in hopes to find one's ticket to heaven? No loving parent in this modern time could honestly agree in this type of 'test' being morally acceptable -even to the most devout Christian it would be greatly unpleasant.

It is these types of books in the Bible that tends to corner even the most honest heart to be selective on what one chooses to believe. However, this is where the *battle within begins*. Shaking the very conscience while forgiving the very flaws in the texts, only sharing a piece of the truth even to themselves through honesty. Unable to escape the reality from truth of the spoken word can be a daunting debate within one's own mind through the fear of the ultimate punishment one is faced with for all eternity.

Because that's what it's about isn't it? Fear -fear of going to a Hellish place for all eternity after one's life here. However, that's how the Bible tricks one into believing to why this is crucial, in order to bestow faith in the 'all powerful God'. If one were to choose the path of disobedience -no matter how outlandish the tests are, it is based on this *fear* that enables the power alone to surrender to these 'tests' of loyalty. It is through this fear of damnation that one is cornered between a rock, and a hard place, metaphorically speaking -that in order to express one's love to the 'higher power', it's necessary to follow and accept all of the contents within the Bible. However, if for any reason you're not fully accepting of it's contents, you're considered a threat to God -thus may receive your eternal ticket to Hell.

An internal debate begins to swerve into play. Asking the questions of:

> 'Have I been loyal enough? Do I love God enough? Will all of my sins (mistakes, shortcomings of perfection) be forgiven? Did I do bad deeds to earn this kind of punishment?'

It's from these questions that originally motivates a person to attend church by openly expressing their devotion. Publicly displaying their faith and shame through active attendance, group activities, or even roaming the neighborhood to recruit in hopes to 'save' others from this same fate. However, it's not to be dismissed as a subtle fling, for even children are faced with these types of questions, even as shy of three years of age.

I'm sure you're aware of Bible study? Bible study is a course that is almost always required in the case of children as well as adults, in order to educate, or better to say -*brainwash* even the most innocent minded. In this case, the child is given no chance of relying on their one wave of thinking, for they're already preserved into the trust that grownups know best. So, being an obedient child, they are too *groomed* into this mindset, and taken into the crude fantasy with the rest of the flock that willingly follow.

If you think your child or any child doesn't think similar levels of fears equal to an adult mind *-think again!* They most certainly do, and are only encouraged to, due to the self-reflections one is peer pressured due to this very kind of medieval ideology. Presumably, the child thus grows into a self-examination where they proceed through life guided by fear, thanks to these exaggerated eternal punishments.

Hard to believe? I don't blame you. However, it only takes a moment of research to understand this reality that is indeed stomach turning. Being that I was raised in a Christian home, it wasn't something I was particularly prepared for -but it's truth nonetheless that people *need* to hear. Sometimes, the truth isn't so comforting, but that's okay because once one is able to understand the facts from the myths, then the process of learning truth *begins.*

THE CONSCIOUS CREATION

It isn't a mystery among the mass collective consciousness nor to the individual, that history has a tendency to repeat itself. Not only in our countries, cities, and traditions but even within our homes and family legacies. More often we tend to miss the mark of the matters that could be easily resolved with simple solutions, if we only took a moment to ponder on the idea of *how* we came to the complicated situations in the first place. The size of the problem is not the matter of fact, but the leading ingredients to *how* it came to be. However, most people are consciously lazy to evaluate certain areas of the human dynamic and instead, throw their hands in the air saying, 'it's beyond our control' -which is the leading cause to why most people skip any amount of responsibility, or accountability for our present dilemmas, or discovering the root of the cause in the first place.

While one may be wondering what religion -the Bible in particular, has to do with the cosmic origin of Demons and other energetic abominations, is for the sake of connecting the dots of the seductive similarities throughout history and human nature. Meaning, to represent the elephant in the room that has been in plain sight since the dawn of dogma was established a great some time ago. For it is in human nature to have a tendency to forget it's consciousness and the capabilities behind it. We as a human, begin to compare ourselves to each other, along with missing the link between us and to what we think we are separate from

-which is another myth I'm about to debunk. It can be easy to simply blame someone else, or something else as to why something bad is happening. This is exceptionally common for those of a Christian faith to point the finger as 'God's judgment' to another as public scrutiny whenever something bad is happening to us -but this is where the finger needs to come down in this scenario.

It is within the cosmology through this structured and distorted religion that connects us to the construction of Demons and Familiars as a whole. However, it is to be wisely noted to remember that this was not done at 'fault', but was the doing from the human consciousness centuries ago that lead us to this galactic spiritual warfare. There is indeed a cosmic (energetic) reason as to why we are in the dealings of these mischievous and not so merciful enemies. Although as it would be simple to state outright, it wouldn't be fair to you, the reader, for then I'd be skipping the construction as to how they came to be. Reason being, religion and the power through *belief* that holds much the origin to how these entities came to be. But it's not to state it was the humans to blame -but it is *how they were created.*

The psychic abilities humans possess is nothing short of *phenomenal.* We as humans are capable of increasing abilities if we only took a minimal amount of time to hone this part of ourselves with absolute belief a day. However, most humans will never use their third eye in their lifetime due to simply being unaware that they possess this capability at all. But it's not always meant as one's path towards personal ascension either, for not everyone is meant to use this ability on their journey -but it's still a part of those nonetheless.

It is with this ability that we hold an exceptional *power* that I used to avoid. In fact, I never was originally comfortable with even using the word 'power' for the first early stages of my life to adulthood. It wasn't until around the age of eighteen did I become aware that we as humans were not alone, which began to uncover truths of where these abilities -such as the third eye comes from.

When one is to accompany a gathering such as attending church on a Sunday, you may be accustomed to hearing someone say, "Blessed be the Lord for he has blessed me." Or another commonly spoken phrase amongst those in the Christian faith is, "The Lord is all knowing and powerful!"

-In this case, that's true -to a careful extent for the *belief* here is where it lies. It's in these moments where I carefully remember the cosmology of us as higher spiritual beings

-yet sadden by the confronting reality that most people still have the unshakable belief that they are never in control of their lives, or of their blessings. As much as there is to say on the many levels to elaborate on that factor alone -to stay on track I will focus on the word 'power'.

Those of a religious belief are almost immediately taught if not soon thereafter, that they are without any type of control of their lives indefinitely. That God is in all control of their life and if one were to ever try to take control of one's life, is only losing faith in the structured design of God, or of the 'higher power'. However, this is where religion fails to institute the cosmology understanding of the human consciousness. Likewise, in Christianity most are gravely instructed not to even remotely, attempt to try to understand oneself spiritually -let alone energetically. However, it's thanks to science that there have been much lessons to guide us through this concept a bit deeper.

As was stated previously in the beginning, you are made up of energy and that energy cannot be created nor destroyed.

Which in turn grants you the undeniable gift of ascension for nothing can or does go backwards, but in fact continues to transcend as it progresses. This progression of us from what I've discovered, not just as a spiritual being, but also as a Psychic Medium is a process to personal conscious ascension. And the self-discovery, or better to say, understanding, has been that we are not without the *same equal capabilities* of this *God* in the Bible.

To elaborate, carefully consider the text that most of us are already aware of. It states in Genesis (1:27):

> *"So God created mankind in his own image, in the image of God he created them; male and female he created them."*

Here is a clear depiction, more so, a *hint* to your energetic cosmological DNA that most people are blind to. This *clearly* states within the Bible itself, that all men and women are created equal to God's image, thus being the *same* ingredients of what is considered *God*. As enormously transformative this is to some -it's also considered the biggest threat to the Christian religion for those are also taught to believe this is what was warned about in *Revelations*. Relatively and respectfully so, I can attest for I felt the same way when I first learned of these words,.. but it equally intrigued my interest all the same. And most people are made, if not enforced to believe that they are limited beings with no power to their own energy of self

-but this is what the religion wants you to believe!

The core construction to religion was to get humanity to be disabled in their own cosmic origin. To remain handicapped of the very ingredient to who we are capable of being. It was religion that made humanity believe for centuries that we are not allowed to take actions into our own hands, nor was it noble to give you the reins to the structure of your own life. There's people to this very day being torn down by their religious belief instructing them that even the simplicity to enjoying music is Demonic -as silly as this sounds, this is people's daily lives.

The majority are influenced by a mass surrounding them with this closed belief that they are nothing without the 'word' guiding them. But not just the word of God, but of the saving of Jesus Christ.

Being 'saved' for one's sins, and worshipping Jesus Christ has been a spiritual belief for centuries, however it was not the structured design nor was it Jesus's wish for people to create their life through this belief. It was not Jesus's original message, nor was it his life's mission to 'save' people from original sin. In short, it was his *passion* to guide those out of this structured religion. In fact, Jesus was labeled as the town's rebellion of organized religion -which lead him to his crucifixion. And in further historical truth, Jesus was not the first 'Christian' -for the very purpose of his teachings was to inspire through the speech of enlightenment through discovering the sense of I AM. He never instructed to orchestrate a ministry but to serve as another messenger through the act of sharing what he had previously taught. It wasn't until many years later the label of "Christianity" came to be. Most Christians that follow this belief are not even aware of this basic historical knowledge - but neither was I for many years. For the church doesn't teach you this -and why not? Because then they would lose power in the church to get you to believe you need this, in order to find salvation from eternal damnation.

How do I know this? I know this not because I read about it, but because I had what's known as a near-death experience at the age of eighteen from a severe allergic reaction to beef. During this time, I found myself greeted by many loving and adoring souls and good vibrations -along with Jesus Christ. He and others explained to me this uncomfortable truth that I'm expressing to you this moment.

The approach I've organized is meant to guide you to how we came to be in this comic warfare with the Demonic. And it was in fact, the harsh implanted religious belief that was the straw, that broke the camel's back. It was the idea, the gut wrenching horror to be damned to a place for all eternity that was only a piece of the puzzle. For it was too the menacing opponent that lay quietly in the night, ready to pounce on the weakest link to collects it's next victim. It was in fact, ***fear of evil*** that was and remains to be the leading ingredient, and culprit to why and how Demons and Familiar entities were created and exist today.

THE POWER OF FEAR

It is ***fear*** that created these sorts of entities, not the religion itself but the fear that was produced from these types of horrific concepts. As hard as this may be to comprehend, let alone believe, take a moment to consider the Law of Attraction. Due to the cosmic nature of our energy being able to attract whatever one wishes -or fears –they are in the creative cosmic process of manifesting that which one is in the focus of with a considerable amount of passion. Due to the passion that emanates enough energy to construct and attract what an individual desires or fears, the universe cannot help but manifest what that individual places their focus on. Because this is so in an individual case -there's no reason to doubt the probability nor the cosmic capability through this Universal Law. If one were to take into consideration this construction and to take a moment to picture millions of people fearing the *same thing*, and the *same time*, then it is only fair to say -that the universe had no choice but to manifest that which we consciously feared *collectively*.

However, it cannot be emphasized enough that it would not be reasonable to place blame on the course of humanity, but to extend the correlation between the human consciousness' capabilities and the universal mechanics behind it.

There is no reason to doubt the sizable impact the emotion fear has on an individual's consciousness. And this is where the emotions from fear have become the factor into how these beings came into existence.

But what does it mean to be within the emotion of fear? To be afraid? There are many fair descriptions when describing fear, but to name a few here are some:

FEAR

Dread, fearful, fright, panic, terror, loss of courage, an unpleasant often strong emotion caused by anticipation or awareness of danger, reason for alarm, danger, Dread usually adds the idea of intense reluctance to face or meet a person or situation and suggest aversion as well as anxiety, Panic implies unreasoning and overmastering fear causing hysterical activity, Terror implies the most extreme degree of fear <immobilized fear>. Apprehensiveness suggests a state of mind and implies a premonition of evil or danger.

It is through the *emotion* of fear that caused Demons and entities to form into creation energetically. The emotion of fear is the second strongest of emotions in the human consciousness, the first strongest is Love. These two emotions are in exact parallel to each other, causing the exact opposite of emotions to manifest that which resonates with that energy. When we go back to the Universal Laws, we can be in a greater understanding of the ability and powerful influence the emotion of fear plays. This is due to us being in the likewise of Godlike capabilities to become the cocreators of whatever one desires -or in this case -*fears*. However, to emphasize, it's not to place blame on humanity for the act of this creative means was not consciously done intentionally by humanity. But instead, was the manifestation that was created from the fear that was constructed and specifically selected throughout history to consciously avoid. It was through the fear of millions of people throughout history, that simply put -created these malicious monsters in the first place.

THIS IS THE INFORMATION DEMONS DON'T WANT YOU TO KNOW

For the moment you know, you are then in the reins of understanding the ability to avoid and even conquer their agenda -which is within the placement of fear.

Exaggeration isn't needed for the very mention of this information was critical to my very life. I've been continually attacked due to overstepping the very bounds that most Psychics Mediums, Demonologists -and even Exorcists are terrified to go. The lengths I've gone through to get this information wasn't something I was even psychologically prepared for. To leave out any amount of mystery, I didn't ask to be attacked, but more so.. I was dealt with facing the undoubtful reality that when one chooses a certain path to truth -must be prepared for how that level of truth will present itself. For the measures of truth are not always going to arrive at one's doorstep in the size one may assume, and this is the lesson I was forced into accepting almost immediately -but I don't regret it regardless of the happenings.

It is this informative concept of fear that allows the person to be more in control of the situation that they may be faced with. The entity's desire and agenda are almost always in the means to impregnate the target with immeasurable amounts of fear to get the person right where they want them. Fear is an emotion that leads a person to either have a fight *or* flight reaction. Entities being fully aware of this human dynamic, they make it their ultimate mission to force the individual to do nothing but become immobilized by the fear that is practically, and sometimes -literally, staring at them in the face.

When one is presented with a moment of fear, they are going to either react in *fight*, or *flight.* Fight, would signify a moment of courage, the act or ability to resist what is being forced upon them. The moment of fearlessness. Courage. However, it's the Demon's agenda to impose you with the idea to act in flight -or to flee in fear which is where they will allow their chances in a greater impact to impress the target with further negative emotions. Here in flight, the moment to try to escape in fear, the Demon, *becomes more powerful* -due to the fact that they feed from the energy of fear.

Because Demons were initially created by the emotion of fear, this is what they energetically crave in order to become stronger and greater in power. Without fear, the Demon would become immobilized themselves, become less of what they were designed to be. This would be fleeting to the entity and would only cause them a level of shame among the other Demonic entities -due to their power level not being as adequate as others. Their level of power is exceptionally important to the Demonic level of consciousness for the more fear they feed from of a human soul, the more resilient they become. It's through fear that the Demonic and Familiar Spirit thrive. They can become greater in their stamina, and even within their transformative methods.

The more one is in a state of fear, the greater the chances of the entity growing in the ability to cause further fear to their human target. This is when a person that is in the state of a series of hauntings will experience extreme levels of Paranormal activity (this will be discussed in a later chapter). Most often the victim of a Demonic haunting will state that overtime the Paranormal activity grew stronger and scarier. This is because the more fear a person grows within their consciousness -it will *psychicly* present an energy signal to the entity to feed from their victim. And the more energy that is being harnessed from the living human target, the stronger and scarier the experiences become. This is where it becomes similar to an abusive relationship -becoming this vicious cycle of neglect and assault that never seems to have an end: The entity causes fear, the human becomes scared, then the entity grows stronger then presents more Paranormal activity -only for the human to get further frightened. The cycle goes on and on only feeding the entity more energy, and more power to terrorize the individual.

People are basically walking antennas with our own energy frequency that is what consists of our soul (consciousness). And this energy of us spiritually, *psychicly* is what the entity drains the living human of, when they are in the process of haunting the individual.

Now that you are energetically and hopefully to say, consciously aware of how these beings came into existence, you're now ready to presume to the next step of learning the types of Demons and what their agenda is. There aren't enough pages to justify the amount of responsibility it takes one to respect, capture a glimpse into the eye of the beast despite the many that suggest this is where the trouble lies. Yes, learning about these entities can partake into the entrance of them becoming attracted to you –*however* that's also depending on the person's state of mind (we will get more into that in a later chapter).

As some believe it's best not to educate oneself on these diabolical forces -I say, it's wiser to know your enemy. For once one is in the *knowing* and cosmic understanding of the Spiritual warfare, they're then given an upper hand to freedom.

*To articulate the leading cause to fear
is from the lack of control,
and it is in this lack that enables the fear
itself to continually grow.
Though the Demon is real, and lively at best,
the entity alone is only a part of the test.
The purest form of challenge to foe,
is the concept of regaining your power to the woe.
Here I stand at the feet of my ultimate Oppressor,
only to discover that fear was the successor.*

Chapter Five

The Malevolent Types

FEAR OF A NAME

Although it's not so proudly practiced, to instruct, nor to remotely speak about these types of forces openly, it's something that *should* be spoken about nonetheless. For the more fear a person has in even talking about these beings, the greater the level of fear is accumulated within the individual's consciousness. Fearing even the name of the beast would only excite the entity more -which is why it's crucial to hold this knowing most definitely. Fear of a name only generates more fear in the very thing itself.

The general public would rather not suggest these types of beings even existing, for the belief is if one were to speak of it through casual mention, will invite the entity into one's life. This is a *myth*. Entities aren't casually to be invited into your life through the simple saying of their very existence, however it does draw their attention. Which is why one must remain aware of their own feelings of the mentioning of the entity, so as to gain ahold of their own conscious energy. But behold the greatest reassurance that it takes much more than just the spoken word to invite this sorts into one's life.

THE IMPOSSIBLE LIST

It has been widely spread by those of a paranormal field to decide it appropriate or soundly 'logical' to publish, much less insinuate that there's a specific name for these types of forces. Or to extend the lengths of reason by suggesting these forces are common -that Demons will simply appear similar like as if in a group of the same type of entity by naming them in a category. -Another thread that must be debunked! For there is an extended ideology being taught amongst 'Paranormal Investigators' that certain entities will always look the same as the other simply because they are within the same 'category' - this is dangerous for there lies the chances of severely underestimating the limitless potential of these negative entities.

Yes, they do come with similar tactics that one can easily place them in a similar category, however to insinuate that these beings have a name and are always to be identified with specific details of their very appearance is naïve at best.

It's been seen and noticed by countless publications where people only being the witness from the outside based on their experience as a human is where this case is critical. It must be carefully, and respectfully noted, that in order for a person to understand the entity definitely -must know the entity cosmically (*psychicly*). Without this ability accepted and honed, the 'Paranormal professional' is only going based on what they experienced as a human, but it takes another level of energy to fully express the lengths of these forces. Without the use of psychic ability, it would be unwise to only remote view the entity's capabilities on just the 'outside' aspect.

As a Demonologist and as a Psychic Medium I've encountered several Demons that not only had different appearances, but their own special skills that were not in the same space as the next Demon. These beings aren't to be labeled into some sort of category of only certain capabilities for this very mindset is what will ultimately and sadly surprise, or shock the person back to a reality check. There is no reason, nor it is logical to suggest these beings are similar to each other. However, their agenda is the only thing that's most often in the likeness of the rest.

Not to say these beings don't tend to appear similar, but to elaborate the importance that these beings are not mostly associated nor to be underestimated solely based on their appearance, or their group like many of these suggestive notions. Demons and Familiar Spirits can appear to have similar features and tactics, but doesn't mean they will hold the same level of capabilities or traits.

THE SHAPESHIFTER

The hysteria that may be whispered about are the features tending to be mutated, or transformed during dream state or other experiences during the encounters.

What does it mean to *shapeshift?* Here is a brief definition for one's own study:

- **SHAPESHIFT:** *One that seems able to change form or identity at will, a mythical figure that can assume different forms.*

  -Merriam–Webster English Dictionary, est 1828

This is to be taken *seriously*, for the very ability for the entity to shapeshift is not to be taken lightly. The very agility to manufacture itself according to it's own liking, is to be understood as an exceptionally excelled opponent. And although this is something to be spoken over, it's also to be noted that these beings crave to shapeshift into the very thing that you fear the most, or likely to fear.

Their very operation of field expectation through the course of succeeding in their agenda is through this technique. If the entity is unable to successfully shapeshift then they are not going to be as successful in reaching their quota of accumulating enough fear energy. So in order to shapeshift, they must learn how to do this through their own skills by the act of adjusting their own consciousness to what they truly desire through their own tactics.

From what I've been able to understand after much deliberation and personal experience is it can sometimes take an entity an exceptional amount of focus in order to conjure their own craft through the target of fear. But all they need in order to accomplish this psychic technique is *you* through the course of *your fear.*

Entities that are able to shapeshift are beings that have done much to practice in order to perfect this skill. But it is not without much distress from the targets they terrorized in order to accomplish this desired skill. Which brings me great dismay, to say if one were to ever encounter an entity with this said ability, then you're most likely in the very eye of a being that would require a said professional to dismantle.

Though this is considered an ability and would be acceptable in the *Advanced Abilities* section, I found it a greater appropriation to mention here for the very ability is not so common for all entities. This is an exceptional gift that only is capable through an advanced Spirit that went through much dedication to get to this point. For this isn't just an ability -but a transformation of it's very appearance where the person that is being targeted could easily be deceived into trusting this sort of 'costume'. It is in this energetic leap where the entity has the upper hand into easily fooling the human target by appearing like a child that is supposedly innocent through an apparition. However, don't be so easily tricked, for the child is no ordinary child, but an intimate scope of deception. Similar to a pervert attempting to kidnap innocence by presenting a sparkly candy with a crooked smile.

THE INHUMAN ASSEMBLAGE

In order to justly comprehend the idea of what one may be dealing with (in case of a haunting) here is a carefully constructed list of the types of inhuman Spirits one may be facing. None should be in the excuse of believing they know everything about the lengths an entity is capable of, for even I do not claim this type of all-knowing. Thus, allow yourself the opportunity to learn as much as you can in order to closely integrate the boundless possibilities. No entity is going to appear, or be exactly the same as the other -which is why it's extremely advisable to not take this list as the only sorts of types you'll be in the dealings with. For their ability to manifest and their capabilities are undeniably irregular, sharp and may arrive without warning!

Below among the names of these sorts of beings will also include the risk factor scale of (1-10). (1) being least threatening to (10) being extreme threat of health complications to even a fatal risk. The danger of the living person's very *soul* existence is at stake and should seek a professional help **IMMEDIATELY!**

⚠

THIS SCALE IS NOT TO BE TAKEN LIGHTLY, BUT SHOULD BE WISELY CONSIDERED FOR YOUR VERY *EXISTENCE* MAY BE AT STAKE.

SHADOW FIGURES

A presence that appears may be similar to like a darkened shadowy figure much like that of a human being. However, this is not to be confused with an ordinary human soul, for this entity is much like a sort of its own, where it holds much hatred towards the living. While attempting to take control of the human's life, it will partake in trickery such as manipulating the person's dreams state, and sucking energy from the living person during sleep state, and even during daytime. Shadow figures can appear in numerous shapes and sizes but to take part in the knowing that these dark figures are so dark in appearance to the naked eye, that it may be impossible to see 'through them'. They will most often appear as an apparition so black in appearance, that it will seem startling to the living. They hold no mercy for even children, for their agenda is to capture and consume a living person's energy. Children and infants are not to be an exception to their agenda. They are capable of moving objects, people, and even to implicate terrible happenings within the person's home or life and even impact the living person's health.

- ✓ RISK FACTOR SCALE **5** – **10**
    These particular entities range between a **5** and **10** due to their personified level of expertise in extracting energy from you and harnessing their own. No shadow figure that one sees should be determined as the same as the other for their very ingredients to disaster are not to be measured the same but on an individual scale.

Poltergeist

A Poltergeist is widely known to cause havoc with levitating objects, people, animals including heavy furniture. Most are under the assumption and are taught from Demonologists and other sources that these are a form of a Demonic force -but *this is wrong*. Poltergeists are indeed a negatively charged entity, however they are not to be confused with the Demon nature for their very cosmology is under a careful construction from the human host. This is right. It is only created and manifested from a living person that is undergoing emotional trauma, severe depression or through other forms of dilemmas that are not being expressed outwardly. Poltergeists are like an energetic parasite, they need a host in order to be created, but cannot manifest nor summed up without a person that is known as a 'Sensitive'. This is a person that is known for having the Psychic ability called, **Psychokinesis.** This is also called, **P.K. Manifestation,** *(Psycho-Kinesis).* This ability is not so common through living humans, so to extend the rarity of this happening significantly, however the entity can still manifest through the living person with this ability. Even if the person is not aware of having this ability, they will still be able to manifest this entity through the course of negatively charged emotions that are suppressed. Thus, the entity cannot survive without the living person extending a hand of energy to this disturbed morphia. The entity would require substantial amount of time in order to linger long enough to gather enough energy to begin creating factual Paranormal activity. The entity will begin to adjust to the humans living with this

person that is the said 'host'. They will begin to feed from their emotions, to cause further negative emotions, thus crafting a vicious cycle of harbored unhappiness that only feeds this negative entity more
-which allows it to then become it's own intellectual creation. Once this occurs, it would require a great deal of professionalism to extract the being out of the galaxy, but not without the host (living person) also going through extensive therapeutic sessions in order for the entity to lose it's power.

The appearance of this being is universal and can transform itself into any sort of shape and or form it chooses. There is absolutely no limit to how these dark beings can manifest.

When it comes to Paranormal activity, they are most commonly known to be violent with an obsession of creating physical disturbances. They are also capable of intercepting into a person's dream state just like a Demon and give the host and other living persons in the same home nightmares. In fairness, this may lead to the assumption that they are 'Demonic' but they are simply able to do the same capabilities but are their own creation that is manifested from the host. Due to the manifestation 'needing' the host, the entity will tag along to the living person's emotions and for the first moments of it's existence will resonate with the host. For example, if the living person is angry or hateful towards a male living in the home, then the Poltergeist will begin to attack the male in dream state or through Paranormal activity. This is not the fault of the living person(s) however, and is to be gravely understood is the manipulation of the entity that is entangled through the emotions of the living host.

In order for this type of entity to become weaker in it's abilities to harm and haunt it's victims, would require the host (living person) to go through extensive therapy. It is exceptionally necessary and *must* be required in order for the entity to be fully extracted from the person's life. The therapy can be a wide range of contemporary measures to allow the living person (host) to become freed from the unsettling emotional baggage. To assist in the lengths of therapy that can be a great game changer for the living person, are some suggested below. Due to each person having their own style to healing, it's customary to remember that there is no right or wrong way to healing, as long as the person is receiving a light of hope to rebuild a sense of self, by releasing these harbored emotions, then the entity will begin to lose grips on said reality.

- Healing through talking to a friend, family member, therapist, or a trusted individual to guide you to healthy steps of healing.

- Writing your emotions down on paper then burning them when ready to release the old to bring in the new.

- Allowing prayer to bring in positive entities to heal and guide you to your next level of love for yourself and others.

- Allow forgiveness to be your guide to letting go of old feelings so as to free yourself from the torture that you may be harboring internally.

- Taking yoga classes to allow one to find their center with other likeminded souls to bring you back to your source of love and healing.

- Taking meditation classes, or meditating in one's own home or personal space of sanctuary with the complete intent to formulate a moment of clarity and peace.

- Attending church or a local gathering that is generated in peace, loving support, and likeminded people to bring you to a sense of safety. *Religion is not required*, nor is a certain faith to bring one to a safe place -but is appropriate if he/she feels it's what they are comfortable with to heal and move forward. Again, no 'right' or 'wrong' way.

- Taking Thai Chi classes to release negative energy and bring in positive energy from the universe through physical appropriation and emotional settings.

- Going to the gym weekly or making a personalized work-out schedule so as to work 'out' the negatively charged emotions that may be weighing on your shoulders and hips. This is extremely helpful when letting go of negative emotions so as to release the feelings through the act of the body. Suggesting through the use of a treadmill, heaving walking, or bicycling in order to move 'forward' and leaving behind the negatives.

Visualizing the act of releasing negativity and bringing in positive energies will bring much success to the living host. This process is expected to take weeks to find solace after the moments of activity from such a thing like a Poltergeist. Patience is required and must be maintained in order to fully evade this emotional, and psychic grip.

- ✓ RISK FACTOR SCALE 3 – 10
    The risk for a Poltergeist begins at a level **3** for the entity is exceptionally rare and is most often due to the living host becoming it's harness for survival. As long as the living person is able to hone and accept personal responsibility (not blame but obligation to this psychic truth), then the living person will be fully freed from ever receiving this type of Paranormal trauma. There is no fault placed on the individual for most often the living person is simply unaware of possessing the Psychokinesis ability. But once one is in full comprehension of this ability, the living human will be allowed to experience a 'normal' life.

Minions, Creatures, Gremlins:
THE TROUBLE MAKERS

There are dark entities in our midst that like to cause turmoil, upsetting situations and even screw with your electronics. I found these names most appropriate for their very agenda is to bring nothing short of bad luck. They will appear similar to a Gremlin, for their very stature is like that of a miniature creature. However, it is also known to spot these creatures in their own appearance similar to that of a Dark Shadow figure, but smaller. The significant difference is their abilities and agenda. They are most likely to be spotted kneeling in a darkened corner, closet or in a hallway. These kinds of entities favor attics, basements, or even under your bed. The very mention of these types of creatures is not to be taken lightly for they are well maintained in letting it all hit the fan.

The profile of their facial structure is universal, but most often I have discovered them to appear with pointy ears with a long sharp nose. However, again, they do appear different from the other for their very appearance can change at will.

It is reported for victims to experience electronics to suddenly erupt in explosions, or shut off without an explanation. Also, to include: fires bursting out of nowhere, floods occur from sources of water, objects to knock over, people to be tripped on occasion, or to arrive home to only discover a mess without a sign of a break in. They fancy the idea of crawling into bed with you, or position themselves directly next to your bed, while staring intensely, which will give the feeling of invasion of privacy. It's not unusual for these dark beings to encourage emotional discomfort by repeatedly banging away on breakables, heaters, and walls.

I personally identify these types of creatures as, your not so average trouble maker, for their very goal is to make your life go up in flames. They are not particularly dangerous, that is depending on the realm they are from, how many there are (some travel in packs) and depending on the level of energy they have accumulated through personal ascension in negativity.

- ✓ RISK FACTOR SCALE 3 – 7
    Minions and Gremlins are leveled at a beginning risk of **3** for their abilities are indeed crafty, but are not to be matched to even a Psychic Medium or a spiritual catalyst. The likelihood of the entities entering your home in multiples is always a possibility which can alter the sense of danger. However, if a person were only dealing with one or two, they are not to be considered an extreme risk but must be removed most definitely. They may try to put up a fight, but with the right amount of help from those experienced in this type of field, you will be allowed back to a life that is free from these sorts of trouble makers.

Earth Bound Souls

Earth Bound Souls are human souls that refuse to leave the earth realm. This is most often due to the lack of interest in ascending away from the vibrations of material experiences here on earth which can lead the soul to lack of love. The type of souls that refuse to ascend are the types of personalities that were not so loving here on the earth realm. This isn't to suggest that all negative types of personalities are stumped in their growth and won't ever ascend to the Other Side, however this does seem to be a commonality for those of a malicious nature. The type of souls that remain on the earth realm are listed below and are listed based on behavioral traits, actions and or agendas.

- **Those that commit murder.** Most often serial killers will desire to remain on the earth realm. This is because when a person commits murder usually once, may find remorse thus grow from this experience. But those that commit multiple murders tend to carry with them accumulated negative emotions/ energy thus begin a desire for further control and to kill again. Most often will even get a 'high' from this type of act which will only encourage the soul to want to do it again, but in Spirit. The likelihood of encountering a human soul that is bound to earth most often is of this nature so their level of danger/ risk is great.

- **Those that molest children.** This is due to the lack of compassion and empathy for the children they do this sort of act towards. Those that commit this crime are endangering the lives of the children they do this to, without empathy for the victims. They tend to carry with them the desire to manipulate with a sense of perversion that prevents the soul from ascending. It may become a surprise to the reader but it's not always something a soul grows from on the Other Side. Humans that coheres a child to do this sort of act on a multiple level with little to no remorse may deal with great challenges of their own ascension. However, it's not to say there's no hope for the types of human souls, for it's an individual standing that must never be compared to another's crime. Each person that does this sort of act will carry with them their own emotions and levels of awareness, and or remorse. If one were to encounter this sort of entity they will most often victimize children or adults that have previously suffered from molestation, rape or other levels of sexual abuse

Being that I'm not a clinical physician, nor am I a psychologist, it's best to remain rooted that the analysis is based on an emotional and an energetic discovery understanding Spiritually.

- **Those that rape or commit other levels of sexual abuse.** These sorts are a greater risk, similar to the types of murdering souls for they have a tendency to crave control by instilling fear into the victim. There are those of this trait in Spirit that will most often remain on the earth realm to encourage other fellow human souls to commit the same acts (or worse!) as they did when alive physically. It's a common trademark for Earth Bound Souls to become underdeveloped emotionally which leads to further peril energetically.

- **Those that were physically or emotionally abusive or expressed excessive amounts of violent behaviors.** These types of human souls will become entranced with the fact they can then trace back to their old habits by staying on the earth realm. They may have been involved in a gang setting, was involved in a volatile cult or group, or may have been involved in being overly controlling by using force and emotional abuse as their tool for control and power. Greed will overtake their very nature in the consciousness and may in fact remember what their desires were on earth and do everything they can to take what is 'theirs'.

✓ RISK FACTOR SCALE **5 – 10**
These types of energies are leveled from a **5** to greater possible risk of the factor scale for this depends on the individual's intentions, goals, and power. The human soul is not limited to be only just what they were on earth, for with in depth practice the human Earth Bound Soul can learn to access further power from other living human souls by the same tactic -using

fear. Fear is their motivation. Human souls such as these will desire control by intercepting into the person's life by invading their sense of privacy. It is to be clear, not all Earth Bound Souls are going to be negative, but the likelihood of the soul that is causing atrocities in the home tend to possess traits that are negatively charged due to their past human life that was most recently lived on earth. For the extraction of a negative Earth Bound Soul, it would depend on the Spirit and of their level of power and agenda. Most often they are not as advanced and are able to be removed from the home with the help of a trained and experienced Psychic Medium, or another form of spiritual counsel. However, if the Earth Bound soul refuses to leave without a fight and is advanced in it's abilities, than the time to seek help in resorting to an *Exorcism* of the property may come to be necessary.

Demons

Demonic energies are not to be taken lightly for the very nature of it's very energetic existence is ravaging. No living human soul is at a match for these types of energies unless they have exceeded certain levels of psychic ascension through extensive meditative practice, Lightwork, and empowerment through the very soulful energy of one's own existence. It's no question the Demonic energy is a worthy opponent, but without giving it credit -it's digestion of choice more often excites only the most diabolical. Demons are known to be the second worst level of energies a human soul may come to face which is one of the leading causes to why they receive so much credit in films and books. However, they are not without dedication for their own target is not of fame, but for the **souls** of humanity. This is one thing religion *does* have correct. Demonic entities crave the human soul with a passion so vile and evasive they will stop at nothing to accomplish their goal.

There are literally countless ways the Demonic entity can manifest, however they are most often experienced as extremely darkened figures or odd shapes that will bring nothing but fear to the human target. A fear so great, so menacing that only doom seems to be within the human's consciousness when these beings are in our midst. Demons don't usually have a gender, for they are universal beings that can manipulate their own embodiment through the energy of their existence. However, there are Demons that do prioritize themselves on an extreme sexual level by manipulating their own appearance that can lead the human target to experience something pleasurable, but rapidly turn into their worst nightmare.

- ### INCUBUS: A SEXUAL MALE DEMON

    The Incubus is within the Demon family for it's commonly identified as a Male Demon that victimizes living females or gay males. This Demon's focus is to take part into involving themselves with the victims sexually. As exciting as this may seem to some, this is in fact the very reason thousands of people suffer due to this powerful desire through the flesh. As exhilarating sexual intimacy can be between two lovers, the experience with a Demon like an Incubus is a ride no one wants to be a part of. For the first initial encounter of this type of entity, the human may experience intense amounts of sexual pleasure that is far greater than the average human experience through physical contact. Although it's seemingly wonderous and quickly addictive, the setting can and **will** change into a *ravage* that the human victim immediately regrets.

The human victim however should *never* be blamed, nor find fault in the matter of enjoying even in the slightest from this experience for that's what the entity does on purpose with the intention to get the person hooked, in order to then attack their prey.

People that have been victimized from this type of experience express pleasure at first but then will find they are being raped in the middle of the night during sleep, and even discover their clothes off after they awaken. Some will express they had lucid dreams of someone coming into their room and interacting with them sexually but then would discover the experience became exceedingly and excruciatingly painful. Such as the feeling of knives stabbing and warping their insides as the being begins to rape or assault them while speaking to them through a tone of perversion. These entities don't target just adults, they too target children even as young as infancy.

- ## Succubus: A Sexual Female Demon

  The Succubus is indeed a trap that tends to elude even the most respected of men and gay women. Their targets are men that secretly hold fantasies, desires that have not be openly expressed or those that crave power through the act of sex. It's common for this type of Demon to appear rather succulent to the male and lesbian. These Demons will announce their presence through the act of giving sexual pleasures to the targets through dream state by allowing the victim to even perform sexual acts to the Demon to encourage increased sexual desire and power through this sort of physical control of the Demon. The Demon will seem beautiful but not in a loving energetic way. More in a sense that is raunchy though the explicit nature of the Demon to get the victim enticed towards this 'fantasy'. But this is their trick that quickly becomes the game of *getting* to becoming the one that is *got*.

  The victims will tend to become entranced by this encounter for a few days to eventually discovering the entity begins to change in intensity to the point they will begin to harm the male or female victim sexually. They will experience rape in a nature that will become exceedingly emasculating emotionally to physically. It will be apparent to the targeted human victim that the velocity of the severity of this spiritual attack will only worsen if not handled and responded to immediately.

> Most however suffer through these terrors alone from the fear of being harshly judged and criticized and even condemned. So to save face, and their reputation, or through the sake of fearing they'd be called 'crazy' - they don't announce the situation until perhaps it's gotten unbearable.

As stated in previous chapters, the Demon is able to manipulate it's own appearance in order to trick the living human target by appearing innocent. Throughout most of the world it's commonly reported where people are experiencing the sight of a young female child walking about certain locations or people's homes. This is particularly crafty yet one of the most activated signs that it's a Demon trying to fool the human target. It's not uncommon for people to be under the misguided impression that the child Spirit is a 'lost soul' -but this is a danger that is incorrect. The reason I know this is through my years of Mediumship, I've come to understand that no child is *ever* left behind in Spirit and are always greeted to go to the Other Side -Heaven. However, the lack of this field knowledge has yet to be taught effectively across the nation, so as to educate those in the Paranormal field to further help other future victims.

 There is hope however. The Demon can only keep this fake identity for very long and will eventually begin to reveal it's authenticity within a matter of seconds, or hours if it desires to do so. Demons don't like to keep hiding for very long for they crave this ability to create fear within the human victims, which is exactly why they don't want to remain in the dark unnoticed. Their goal is to gather energy of human souls for the soul energy is exceptionally powerful, and fresh for the Demon to collect, but it's through this simple trick that gives them an unfair advantage. It is through this act and countless others that Demons are then able to enter the human target's physicality and take over through the act of, **Influence** and **Possession** -which will be discussed in a later chapter.

- ✓ RISK FACTOR SCALE <u>8 – 10</u>

    Demons are the second highest level of risk which is why they are leveled at **<u>8</u>** on the scale. There are no other words to say, but to express without hesitation, that no person should take this lightly. If you or another person you know feels are under the attack of a Demonic force -must seek Demonology counsel *immediately!* Demonic entities work closely with other Demons, and they most often are under the order of Devils. These sorts of Spirits are not one to show mercy and should be gravely understood are not to be trusted under *any* circumstances.

Devils: descended masters

Demons are not so unusual to encounter believe it or not, however it's the Devil vibration that I've come to find is a rarity of it's own. Granted, the likelihood to evaluate and to discern the authentic Demon haunting is factual, however, there are still more Demon hauntings than there are of the actual Devil status. This is due to the hierarchy that establishes the Devil's agenda through acting as the controller for the lower vibrational entities, like Demons. Devils most often won't do their own dirty work, so will likely arrange the Demon to do the Devil's bidding.

It's commonly believed that there is only one Devil entity -most especially taught in the Christian religion -however this is also a wide spread misconception. The uncomfortable truth is there is not one Devil creating havoc on the land of earth, but there are indeed *many*.

The Devil energy is so invasive, with an intense motivation to annihilate the human race, that they will stop at nothing to see their objective in succession. The reason this is so, is due to the reality that because energy is always evolving and changing, so are souls/ Spirits on the Other Side. Just like Angelic beings being allowed to evolve and grow, so can Demons. Once a Demonic entity has reached a certain level of respectable energy and ability to take the reins, the entity is then permitted the opportunity at being basically promoted. This is not to be confused with something like receiving an award of grace, but is to be established only through the Demon remaining subservient, and enslaved for centuries while committing heinous crimes.

Devils can appear and behave similar to the Demon entity, however they are extremely adaptable, powerful and are solely for the human *soul* and very *existence.* Their very goal is to suck a human's energy to the point that the person no longer *exists*. When I first learned of this, it was something of a shock indeed.

Which is why the victim's soul is ever so precious and vital during an Exorcism. For the entity isn't trying to steal the human's *existence,* but ultimately annihilate it for the purpose of further power.

The presence of a Demon is similar to the inherited cringe of a serial killer, but the Devil's energy without requiring action of the killer, permeates the active ingredients to what makes that serial killer. Inside the Devil's cosmology is only noted to be the luxurious barriers of unhappiness, doom, sadness, and fear with the lack of hope. The moment a Devil were to come into the room or much less the area of a location, any, and all other entities cower in fear for the power can destroy their exact existence.

- ✓ RISK FACTOR SCALE <u>10</u> (SOUL DANGER)
  The risk factor measurement of a Devil entity begins at the highest level of danger for the human victim's very soulful existence is at stake. Though Spirits are not limited to the concept of time on earth, they don't like to waste their chances regardless of how many opportunities are presented. Diablo, The Angel of Darkness, Satan, or Devil doesn't matter what you call these diabolical beings but what they do is all the difference. Extracting a human's very existence by delivering menacing maneuvers is one of their masterful ways of succeeding in their goal. These dark forces are what I also consider to be Descended Masters from their apathetic nature energetically.

They are considered the most negatively charged force one could ever come into contact. Thus, requires a team of exceptionally trained, and experienced Demonic professionals in the field -for not even religion or your faith can save you. No human soul is a match for a Devil unless is highly advanced in their spiritual journey with Ascended Masters and Spirit Guides. This is where prayer of help from other higher Ascended beings is a *must*.

Familiars

Familiar entities are a bit more complex and are not to be confused with the habitual traits of a Demonic Spirit. Familiars are a form that is manifested from either a P.K. Manifestation *(not all P.K. Manifestations are going to be the likeness of a Poltergeist)*, or from a conjuring method through the act of magic. Entities of this nature are more so Spirits that are concocted from a living human person that is in the occult such as Voodoo, Witchcraft (dark magic) or other levels of sorcery that is designed to take revenge, or to control through the emotion of anger and hatred. This is not to identify these sorts of occult practices as 'evil' but to simulate the energetic formations that can be constructed through these types of spiritualisms. It's not the practice that identifies one in the nature of 'dark' (negative) or 'light' (positive), instead it is through the act and the intention of the individual that deems this so. As nature is both loving and cruel, so are the practices based on the one participating willfully. It is in the internal psychic decision of a person to decide to wish in the thoughts of love or in the thoughts of revenge and hatred. It is from the human's emotional database the will create either a positive entity or a negatively charged one. With this in mind, Familiar Spirits are also not limited to their potential, and are very much alive and active when they are being guided and order through the living human host. These sorts of entities most often don't have a will of their own in the beginning, however, overtime the entity will gain internal energetic access to their own personality, thus may establish it's own level of intelligence, becoming aware of it's own existence. This can then allow the entity to retaliate and even attack their creator to break the bond.

- ✓ RISK FACTOR SCALE 1 – 10

    In order to properly determine the risk factor of a Familiar entity is for the Psychic Medium, Demonologist, or other Spiritual Counselor to closely examine the situation and the entity itself. These sorts may become excessively violent, or they will be non-aggressive beings that one would barely know is there, unless the entity made itself known intentionally. Most often a Familiar entity can be treated with proper cleansing techniques of your home, property, and of yourself. The entity only has so much power depending on the intentions and passions that were originally harvested by the living person that created this being. When one is in the suspicion of facing a

Familiar spirit, mustn't panic, but should seek proper counsel if the experience of this type of entity has indeed gone to a level of physical touches, Paranormal activity, nightmares, or sexual/ physical violence.

THE UNPARALLELED APPARATUS

It's best to acknowledge a cosmic understanding that Demons are in fact their own breed of creation *individually*. To explain, I've recently discovered after terrors of my own as a Medium and with the help of my Spirit Guides, that Demons are not to be mistaken as one like the other. Yes, Demons do approach humans in a similar pattern -but their traits, characteristics and appearance are not to be assumed as the same as the rest. In fact, I was heavily instructed by my Master Spirit Guides that Demons are their own identity, that one Demon entity by it's very self, is to be understood as *it's own creation* that is personable to the energetic vibration of it's very existence. They are all a slave to their very vibration, and to the core aspect of their purpose of living, which only permeates the root causes to their style of approach.

Chapter Six
Knock Knock: Infestation

HOW THEY ENTER

Negatively charged entities and energies can enter into a person's life in nearly countless of ways due to the Universal Law of Free will. However, the most spoken misconception within the Christian faith is the thorough belief that these sorts of energies can only infest into a person's life when they personally invite the entity.

This is **completely false.**

Entities do not need to be formally invited into one's life to cause hell for the living victim, for all it can take is simply being at the wrong place at the wrong time. Demons and negative Spirits have their own intelligent consciousness, thus are free to make the conscious decision to invade into a living person's life or not. However, many people state the false belief that Demons don't possess Psychic abilities

-where they got this myth, I don't know. But as an advanced Psychic Medium with extensive supernatural experiences with Angels, Spirit Guides, Higher beings such as Jesus Christ and including Demons, I've learned that all beings in the universe have Psychic Abilities -including Demons. This is because we are all able to read the energies, for that's what Psychic Abilities are: a range of conscious skills that allow the entity to 'read' into past, present, and future. And the way these dark monsters can infest into a living person's life is through numerous amounts of ways that may seem harmless at first, but roughly transform into something ruthlessly menacing.

The purpose of my work is not just to inspire but to help protect and defend those that may be in this situation. However, in order for this book to be deemed successful, I had to first test my theories, methods and the concepts through studying the Demon's strategies. This information wasn't established from a collaboration of other author's work, nor from conformed belief systems. The very concepts of the entities was constructed from facts based on the experiences I've had, and my client's.

These ways that are listed below on how a Demon or a Familiar Spirit enters one's life, is through a series of strategies that enable the entities a higher chance at success. It is through the consistency that presented these conclusions to how these types of Spirits invade into your life with full force. No human is exempt from the clutches of the darkened culprit, however some may presume they are 'untouchable' to dark forces. I must relay with extreme caution through granting awareness - these entities do NOT have an 'untouchable' list. All human souls are a potential target and are not to be measured based on a belief system or through external measures: race, sexuality, traditions, belief systems, culture, age, or gender. The very dynamic of the Demonic trait is to target the least likely of human targets. But if one were to ask,

How do humans become targets, and why?..

..then one must proceed to the following for that very answer.

Séance Ritual

Through a Séance people will create a circle by sitting at a typical round table, or may sit cross legged on the floor, while having lit candles in the middle of the arranged circle of participants. Some may prefer numerous candles presented among the room that is being used for the ritual. The séance itself is not to be determined evil or ill intentional, for the participants most often entertain the idea of befriending a Spirit that is either 'lost', or simply wishes to connect with a departed loved one. However, this very ritual is what creates drama within the circle of participants that engage in this type of practice. The naivety is typically guided along the reins with someone that may be perceived as in the 'knowing' of these sorts of practices, but rapidly the outcome after the ritual may adjust into something negatively charged. It's commonly reported those that openly participate in the ritual of a séance will discover that the person in charge may have gone too far. Expressing the Psychic Medium that very well may be guiding along the ceremony will perceive to be behaving rather strangely, out of his/ her character. Some express the person that is instructing the ceremony attempts an open Possession, by allowing the entity that is projecting to take part through communicating with the group by influencing or Possessing the willing individual.

This must be said with haste -*any person that chooses to openly become Possessed or Influenced by the entity is not corresponding rationally, nor wisely, and is subject to full Possession most definitely.* No matter how advanced a Psychic

Medium is, nor how confident one may seem, it's to be deemed unwise and is considerably irresponsible of that individual for they are putting their very *soul* and other's lives in jeopardy.

Though the practice of a séance is risky enough, the very suggestion from someone to partake in a Possession or a Spiritual Influence willingly -is most often subject to also encouraging further irrational decisions. These sorts of individuals must be taken seriously and should in fact be spoken out of the remote idea, much less even participate, for their logic alone has not analyzed the dangers thoroughly. It's advisable, if one ever partakes into this type of ritual, be sure to speak with all of those involved in the séance to have guidelines of what is allowed and not, for the safety of each person depends on the individual decisions throughout the entire ceremony.

During the séance there will be interactions and questions asked during the ceremony. However, the unfathomable reality that most 'professionals' miss is the fact that even if the person in charge, or the group were to make rules to the Spirits engaging, it must be noted that they won't listen to you - ***period***. Just like any other practice, one cannot tell what another soul can or cannot do, thus the very belief that one can instruct an entity orders during a ritualistic practice is gravely mistaken and misguided. No entity on the Other Side (afterlife) can be controlled, and will do what they please regardless of the séance's 'orders' or regulations.

During a séance the group may in fact remain aware of their surroundings while receiving some level of Paranormal interactions with a Spirit during the ritual. They may indeed be told by the entity that they are 'safe' and or are not a Demon. But this is again another misguided assumption. Demons and Lower Vibrational energies that remain on the earth realm most often are deceivers and will lie to you to gain your trust. This is why it's not inherently a wise practice when partaking in a séance for the very potential of running into a Demonic, or negative Earth Bound Soul is not only highly possible, but *almost always* a guarantee. The very position of people formed into a circle creates what's called a **Portal,** and this portal enables the souls from the Other Side among millions, and billions of galaxies away from us to hear this initiation and will participate if desires. The portal is created through the psychic energy that is accumulated from the participants that are arranged in the ceremony's circle. Most participants are not even aware that their very presence in the ritual ignites the very energetic signal to create the portal that thus enables the entities to hear the **Call.** The call is the telepathic communication that is done through the very intention of the people involved in the séance. One doesn't have to speak out loud to communicate with the entities during the séance, all that is initially required is the intention and the psychic energy to manifest this open communication.

The other misconception a séance ritual, is people think that if they participate the séance in an abandoned building that the entities engaging are bound to that specific location. I cannot tell you how many people I've encountered that expressed their misunderstanding and judgments of the power of a séance. Countless clients and even people I've randomly encountered would share their length of communication with the Spirits during a séance only to unfortunately discover the entity then followed them home. This common, unfortunate truth is many people still believe in this myth that must be shattered.

The risk for an entity to follow the participants home -even across the world after a séance is towering. Although there are levels of cleansing one may preform, in order to ward off negative energies, the risks are still a reality that one must face when willingly conducting such a ceremony like a séance.

Cursed Objects and Conduits

It is widely known that objects can become cursed or used as a form of a conduit that which gives the false impression of a Demonic possession. Though it may appear suitable to assume that a moving object such as a doll or other things become Possessed by evil forces, however this is a widespread misunderstanding. Such a decent example would be the Annabelle doll that was being used as a conduit with a Demonic entity in order to gain trust and further ability to create hell to victims. You may have heard of this from the famous film, The Conjuring where Paranormal Investigators, Ed and Lorraine Warren, took part in the case. Ed being a well respected, and acknowledged Demonologist, and Lorraine known for her exceptionally skilled Clairvoyant abilities were a dire need in order to help the families and victims. Not only is this a savory case to take careful consideration in, but a classic one. For the very nature of Demons is not to Possess items, but to trick people so to be invited into the victim's life without being the wiser. The concept to understand with Demons is they don't Possess items that are either cursed, or that are a potential conduit. Instead the Demon is energetically attached to the chosen item, so as to catch their next victim by manipulating the item in order to strike impending doom to their victims.

However, a cursed item very well may only be a form of something like bad luck, losing money, ill health, or bad dreams, or something as intense as condemning the person to a fatal fate if in possession of the item. Cursed items essentially are objects that a living person manipulated with their own Psychic energy along with any other supernatural help from other forces from the Other Side. With this, the cursed object can inherently attract negatively charged entities.

Witchcraft and Wicca

In the practice and religion of Witchcraft and Wicca is a strong connection to the universal energies and nature. It is to be carefully understood that the practice of Witchcraft is not in the same likeness of the belief of Wicca. Wicca is a religion and Witchcraft is a practice. Not all Witches are Wiccan, nor are all Wiccans Witches. The focus of Wicca is on the Lord and Lady, the Wheel of the Year, and one's spirituality. The focus of Witchcraft is on the casting of spells (magic) and the use of herbs towards a specific end or result. Arguably, a Wiccan can still be identified as a Witch if the person were to take part in spell casting, herbs, or conjuring spirits on the Other Side for one's bidding. The determination of one being a Wiccan or a Witch is solely based on one's interpretation for what constitutes a religion. There is also a wide debate that one may start out as a Wiccan focusing on the spiritual connection of the deities and the energies, but then slowly gravitate towards the practice of spells and even curses. If this is the case of the Wiccan, then the Wiccan has indeed turned towards the craft of Witchery.

There is absolutely no need to identify nor to connect Witchcraft or Wicca to Satan worship. This is another *myth* and a rumor that was spread like an angry disease from the Catholic and Christian faith centuries ago. Devil worship is not the same and wouldn't be fair to totally label them to this sort of shallow thinking.

However, the dangers through Witchcraft and Wicca remain a vital urgency due to the individual's intention. Neither Witchcraft nor Wicca are evil nor are they to be suggested as so, but it is to be mentioned with duel sensitivity that both are just as able to become harmful if not used or practiced wisely. For it is through the person's intention that creates the 'evil' from the religion or the practice. I've met plenty of Witches and Wiccans and neither are to be labeled 'bad' for it's not the belief that creates an evil person but the intention behind and through their actions. This would be no different than to say, a police officer is always to be trusted, for this alone is not to be true for there are plenty of people in the police force that go rogue and do things to abuse the power they were privileged to wield. Thanks to centuries of negative Christian agenda, it's indeed scarred the honest reputation of many in this sort of practice and spiritual belief unfairly.

Those in this spiritual belief or practice are not automatically a target to Demonic and Familiar energies and this must be digested. It is in the intention of the individual and what they do that evolves the person towards a negative entity or not.

I've received letters from individuals who were in the belief of Wicca but then began spells to take revenge on another person. Through this sort of act, one is designing a **Karmic** repercussion towards even themselves for the revenge cannot go without a balance coming back around. We exist in a universe that is the sum of energy that resonates with like energy -this includes through actions and intentions. Once a person is using the craft to articulate their negatively charged intentions, those intentions then become a reality causing harm to those they targeted. Although this may seem like a harmless act, the underlining fact is these *causes* from the spells don't just happen from the caster, but from other entities that are also granting those wishes, desires or curses. The Witch or Wiccan that is partaking in these spells doesn't have to be consciously aware that the dark forces are making the spells a reality, for they don't need the approval. All they is for the living caster to believe that it's working, and to know they can keep doing it. Once they are fully aware of the spell's magical outcomes, this entices the human caster to perform other forms of spells and or curses. This is what catches the Demon's eye for they want you to go against your morals. The negatively charged entities are naturally drawn to those that are more susceptible to dark behaviors -like curses, greed, control, or revenge.

It is to be noted that Witchcraft and Wicca are only a risk for negative Spirit encounters if the individual were to conjure or to preform spells for evil. If one were to steer clear from this sort of ego driven agenda, then one most often will suffer not from these negative forces.

Paranormal Investigations

Those that partake in Paranormal Investigations are most likely to receive the supernatural backlash. The reason this is, is due to the locations the investigator will engage their investigations in. The common belief is Paranormal Investigators are professionals in the field of paranormal activity and are well grounded in the understanding of entities. This is true, but *only* by individualism. However, I can tell you from years of my own experiences with many people that engage with Spirits in this manner most often don't know nearly enough basic information on the entities and of the severity. In fairness, as a Psychic Medium the use and need of Paranormal Investigators is crucial and is indeed helpful to allow closure and validation to the locations and the victims. Except to accept the humility that one must take into the considerable reality, that if the Paranormal Investigator doesn't possess either a Psychic Medium, or are not intuitive enough themselves through their own abilities -they might as well be children playing hide and go seek in the dark.

The necessity and rooted purpose for Paranormal investigations were created to allow the victims a chance at retrieving credible proof that their client's home was haunted. To give the victims a sense of validation that they aren't going 'crazy'. There are thousands of Paranormal Investigation groups conducting 'investigations' right now, but instead of going to people's homes to help identifying the haunting problem, they are going to abandoned locations that don't need to be investigated. This is not only pointless, but is only pissing the entities off which is one of the major factors to why many of the investigators end up being followed and haunted themselves. This sort of reality is also one of the leading causes to why many Paranormal Investigators stop the investigations all together. This is unfortunately due to the individual underestimating the likelihood of also too becoming a target.

It's not unusual to hear of an individual that is engaging in a Paranormal Investigation to push the entities to challenging them. I've witnessed in certain Paranormal groups attempt to take the negativity to a whole other level by daring even Demonic entities to attack them -just to prove their existence. Most people may genuinely see this sort of act as brave, in order to prove the afterlife exists. But if you wanted my honest feedback: dare I say, -it's one of the most ignorant moves a person can make. I say *'ignorant',* due to the lack of full awareness of the capabilities these entities can presume. And when the person does get attacked, all I can equally say is they asked for it. As insensitive as this may seem, I'm a harsh realist, and I strive to tell it like it is. If one were to ask to be hit by an invisible, yet by an immeasurable powerful force, then you only have what's coming to you to teach you what is wise.

To place blame on those that have had this experience would be insensitive to the truth of their desire to help others, or to prove the supernatural existence. No person should be blamed for this sort of happening. However, it is without pleasure to be the bearer of bad news that most often those that engage in Paranormal Investigations and become another human target is *nearly absolutely promising.*

Ouija board or Talking board

Through the use of a Ouija board or also known as a Talking board, a person is given the ability to communicate with Spirits through this empty device. As innocent as this game may appear, it's roughly one of the most common devices used and quickly regretted.

It's a terrible reality that these boards are sold in our local stores and targeted toward children as young as eight years old. These boards are encouraged by the toy companies that they are an imaginative board game equally fun for the entire family. But without the mystic understanding and with equal respect of these supernatural forces, they quickly have become one of the most dangerous and famous of ways in contacting the Spirit realm.

The ability for the Demonic and Familiar forces to engage and interact with humans, is similar to the ways of a Séance. It all depends on the individual's intentions, but no matter how safe one attempts to be during these sorts of ceremonies, will never guarantee a positive experience nor outcome. For it is Lower Vibrational Spirits that are motivated by greed, hatred, power, and control that most likely come through the board. This is due to knowing and understanding as a Psychic Medium that Higher Vibrational Spirits won't come through a board most often simply because they've excelled passed the earth realm. Spirits that leave the earth realm for a time to ascend in love will easily connect with their living loved ones in ways such as dreams, animals, children and even through Psychic Mediums, so the purpose of a Ouija board is not usually needed nor is it preferred.

Being an Awakened Person

Simply by being one that is recently 'awakened' or a person that is known as a *Lightworker,* or a Psychic Medium are unfortunately prone for the rest of their human days to being walking targets for Demonic and unfriendly Spirits. If unaware of the meaning and purpose of a **Lightworker:** *it's a person that chose to reincarnate on earth with a soulful contract to help guide, heal and express the higher levels of love, compassion, and kindness.* Near-death experiencers are too known for experiencing said dark encounters with other sorts of beings that follow them, speak to them, or try to cause harm to them at home or at other locations.

The reason this is, is due to the undeniable Spiritual connection to the Other Side that which encourages other Spirits to take a greater notice to them on the earth realm. If you were to imagine all of the people in the world suddenly becoming stars, and those stars having their own lights. Maybe some are different colors, or different levels of brightness. It's in this light that those awakened Spiritually will be more targeted due to their light tending to be energetically brighter than others. Not to insinuate that brightness means more love of God or more love from that person. But to initialize a cosmic understanding that once a living person reaches a certain point of consciousness their 'light' thus grows along with their own awareness. And it's within this light of awareness that antagonizes and enriches the Demon's desire to attack those specific people with specific energetic abilities.

The other reason is because people that are awakened are more naturally intuitively aware of the change in energy at locations and within people. This awareness with their advanced intuition grants the Demon what it wants
-attention. And with this awareness to change in energy, the Demon is able to frighten the person more, which then means, more energy (power) for the Demonic and Familiar Spirit.

Granted, all people are and possess Psychic Abilities just like other beings on the Other Side, however some are more awakened and aware of this ability than others, due to a conscious amnesia that causes most of the human race to continue life completely blind to their cosmic origin, and abilities.

S̲tudy of D̲emonology

Merely studying the concepts of Demons and Familiar Spirit enables the entrance of darks forces to enter one's life. Of course, there is nothing more sacrificial than the choice of an Exorcist or a Demonologist to do everything in their power to learn of these malicious entities in order to relieve those of their mangling grips. This study is not one that should be taken lightly for the very conscious moment to initialize this study enrages the Demonic forces, for their motivation is to purposely stop and even annihilate their foes.

Demons and Familiars become Psychicly aware of the person's intentions of studying their cosmology and abilities without struggle. From this awareness of us alone, allows every single Demonic entity and Familiar to remain fully entranced with the human they're feeling may become a threat to their very agenda. This includes the malicious Descended Master Devils along with other likeminded energies.

When driven to do the unthinkable, which is to face one's ultimate enemy that is created through fear, the very mention of Demonology is not a life a person ultimately wants. The common spiritual and religious belief however, is this course of professionalism is not chosen by the human, but that it was chosen by God. This is only partially true. We are all made in God's image (the universe's image) which ultimately defines that the human souls are ultimately in charge of what they choose to pursue. The 'God' that chose to fulfill this purpose was in fact the Demonologist and Exorcist himself or herself. This is not out of the person's hands like many belief systems portray. It's the individual's choice. To thoroughly understand this concept, one must be willing to get themselves out of the box that is labeled 'dogma'. No human soul if forced to pursue a purpose they don't want to journey through. Instead it's to be understood that each soul that is driven to help humanity in this way, is from their soul deciding to before incarnating or reincarnating on the earth realm.

It is in the individual's divine purpose of this life is to help guide, and to potentially protect those that become victims and to hopefully prevent these attacks from happening. However, the Demonologist and Exorcist are not untouchable, for their very life is in danger regularly, while working to prevent these beings from raiding your home and very existence.

Alcoholism or Drug Abuse

When an individual relieves one's stresses of the day with a casual cold beer or with your favorite wine, there is no harm nor shame in this human luxury. Although, it is when the person turns towards this lower vibrational high a little too often, that may arrange a greater interest in the Lower Vibrational Entities like Demons and Familiars. Likewise, the course of the intake of over the counter drugs for the cure of a headache or even a pain reliever that was prescribed from your doctor post-surgery, isn't to be shamed over. However, after a certain level of consumption the person's consciousness will experience a shift in awareness and judgement, which is what draws the Spirits towards the person more. For after a certain amount is consumed and is taking a negative effect on the mind, and soul, the psychic abilities naturally heighten as the person's instinctual guard begins to go down.

This may cause a person to undergo negative experiences such as having terrible headaches that are not typical from the substances used. May experience awkward dreams, and even nightmares that cause the person to awaken from sleep screaming, even to discover inexplicable bruises, scratches, or scars. The individual may become more aggressive from the toxins after over consumption of their substance of choice.

A Demon's desire to raid the home of the unsettled and to target their already unhappy emotions like disappointment, guilt, fear, doubt, or regret. This would also include those that become abusive from the drug or beverage of choice. It is in the motion of anger that only antagonizes these emotions which is exactly the motivation from negative entities. When the home or environment becomes violent, neglectful, or abusive physically, or emotionally, the entity becomes stronger and more powerful, thus granting the dark Spirit a more higher chance at success by destroying the love and hope in the victims within the home.

Not to place blame, nor shame on those that may be struggling with the disease of alcoholism, or drug addiction, but the risks from becoming negatively impacted from the Demonic beings inherently heightens. The discomforts from being drawn to an addiction without full control is ravaging of the soul all alone, but to include the statistical odds of too becoming targeted by negatively charged entities admittedly adds to the stress.

There is hope here however, for as long as one is in the process of seeking help from trained professionals, there is a light at the end of this seemingly darkened tunnel of misery. After a few weeks of one obtaining and maintaining sobriety, the individual will begin to feel brighter, lighter energetically and emotionally. The Demonic entities strive and strike on those that potentially have a weakness. And as sickening as this is to stomach, the unfortunate reality that one must face with courage, that in order to break free from their clutches, is by the power and choice of one's own free will. By overcoming the malevolent mutilation through one's free will, is to resist the temptation, or better to say, the ugly triangle of unhappiness.

Demon Tarot and Ouija

The use of a Demon Tarot deck or a Demon Ouija board are without question -*hazardous*. Those that intently use these types of occult devices to purposely connect with Demonic energies are only in the comings of a rude awakening. Some that are in possession of these empty vessels more often, than not, arrange for the summoning of a Demonic entity with the intention to harm another person, gain power, control or for even the purpose to receive obscene sexual stimulation. It's this irrationality that begins to consist of acute Demonic and Familiar attacks not so long after the initial conjuring. Lacking in the moral high ground, some individuals may choose to interact with the Demon by agreeing to become enslaved in the afterlife, if the Demon were to do the conjurer's bidding. Some may extend this madness to selling their very soul for his or her fantasies to become a reality. In short, nothing good stems from the use of these devices.

-

The use of a Tarot deck is not to be measured or assumed as only used for evil, for there are Angelic decks that are used by Oracles, Psychic Mediums and so forth. Tarot itself is neither good nor evil, for it is determined based on the one that is using the deck. It is through the person's intention that may initiate a positive or a negative experience, for Tarot is not solely to communicate with other worldly Spirits, but for the guidance from the person's intuition of which card is next in line for one's cosmic answers to their questions.

-

Wrong place, Wrong time

It's been reported not only across the United States, but throughout the world where people will move to a new home with excitement, only to soon uncover a dark guest that looms the halls. This happens more often than some are usually accustomed to hearing for the moment a home becomes haunted by an unclean Spirit, the residents of that space often will leave the premises as soon as possible. Once the prior homeowners move to a new home, at times the entity will stay in the now, evacuated home, awaiting the arrival of the new tenants.

Here, the entity is able to find a suitable pleasure in regaining a personal space on earth, but when new owners move into the house, the Demonic entity will feel invaded. Demonic entities are known to be extremely territorial for gaining control in their chosen space is their primal instinct. Once a family or person(s) move into this space that is when the terror soon arises causing another course of catastrophe.

The attention from a spirit that is full of hatred may also become a person's reality after or during a moment of being in a new location. Simply by visiting a location that is neither abandoned or condemned is subject to the possibility of encountering other worldly terror. This would include homes, apartment buildings, business buildings, restaurants, bars, stores, and even hotels. To note: negatively charged entities are often drawn to negatively charged locations: if it's a bar, it may be a bar that is known for a lot of violence and death. It's not so much the location itself the entity is drawn to, rather the history, and what's known as **Residual Energy.** *Residual Energy is an energetic memory that's been implanted within the location from where trauma has taken place.*

It is in this Residual energy that encourages further negativity unless the area and the people impacted are cleansed thoroughly.

Satanism and other Occults

The practice of Satanism, Voodoo and others, unfortunately often end up down a blackened path. In these sorts of belief systems and ritualistic practices, require some levels of sacrificial ends in order to see their desired results from their practices. *Voodoo* is a black religious cult practiced in the Caribbean and the southern US, combining elements of Roman Catholic ritual with traditional African magical and religious rites, and characterized by sorcery and Spirit Possession.

Whereas Satanism has several types of its own levels of beliefs. *LaVeyan Satanism* for example, is a new religious movement that was founded in 1966 by the American occultist and author, Anton Szandor LaVey. The religion's doctrines and practices are codified in LaVey's book, The Satanic Bible. Its core philosophy is based on individualism and egoism, encouraging an epicurean pursuit of fleshly indulgence and an eye for an eye code of ethics. Then there is *Theistic Satanism* which is the belief that Satan is a supernatural being or force that individuals may contact and supplicate to, and represents loosely affiliated or independent groups and cabals which hold such a belief. Another characteristic of Theistic Satanism commonly includes the use of ceremonial magic.

No Satanist is to be identified as the same for there are different beliefs of Satanism respectfully. Though I am grounded in the respect that each soul is meant to follow his or her own path without judgment, those following in this type of belief is set to make an encounter with dark forces *incredibly*. However, not through the simplicity of the belief does this cause the entity's curiosity of the human target, but through the deepest desires and core ideologies of the individual. For each person hold's their personal levels of beliefs regardless of the identity they've branded themselves with through the choice of their religion.

Demonic energies are drawn to those that are drawn to egoism, thus the likelihood of becoming intensely and closely examined from the diabolical. Though not all followers in these religions will be drawn to this particular path, but some may become entranced with the insatiable craving for power, money, sex, control or other means by preforming unfathomable ceremonies that may require animal or even human sacrifice. As salacious as this may sound, the truth is in the documented news reports from those committing heinous crimes in the name of Satan or for another dark purpose. For those that crave power may become capable of even the most menacing of actions imaginable when clouded by the cloak of vanity and greed. Some have gone to the lengths of kidnapping or even sacrificing their own newborn babies, for the person committing these crimes themselves cannot resist the urge to create a change through the actions of these rituals. It's as if their whole person has vanished and was replaced with an apathetic creature that is not accustomed to humanity's morals and innate mercy.

Of course, it's unwise to suggest that *all* those that follow the belief of Satanism are prone, or even agree in these sorts of dark rituals, and shouldn't be automatically judged as so. For these cases as rare as they come and are a painstaking cringe to the religions and shouldn't be labeled in a general sense.

Some are under the impression these practices are against God -Christianity is a solid believer in this interpretation. However, it's neither good nor evil of the choice of religion one wishes to follow, but it's the person's innate desires, rooted beliefs, and core energetic DNA that is what makes something good or evil. Just like nature, wind is neither good nor bad, but it's based on the impact the wind makes in the moment that creates this sort of impression. The right question, or better to say, confession, is whether one likes to admit it out right or not -there indeed seems to be a dim force at work when an individual dives deep into the rabbit hole of power and ego.

FOR THE SAKE OF KNOWLEDGE

Learning about the ways a Demonic Spirit can enter a person's life is not to be limited to only what was mentioned, but to be used as a carefully examined guide. The possibilities of Demons and Familiar Spirits entering a person's life are nearly limitless, but for the sake of knowing, it's best to advise one to take a moment to internalize what's been learned. Though the education of these malicious beings can bring the entity towards you, be reassured the only chances of that becoming your reality is if you were in the moment of deciding to purposely learn, protect others, and to educate the Demonic nature as a Demonologist, Psychic Medium, an Exorcist or as another from of a Spiritual Catalyst.

Demonic beings are not without a full level of their own intelligence and free will. They are not to be considered robotic beings without a choice in those they choose to follow and haunt or not. It does bring the Demon great pride for their goal is attention, for the greater the fear the further the power the entity may assemble. Except, this isn't a matter of gratifying the demonized, but to accept it's possible entrances and lengths to it's full potential.

Chapter Seven

The Disturbance Begins: Oppression

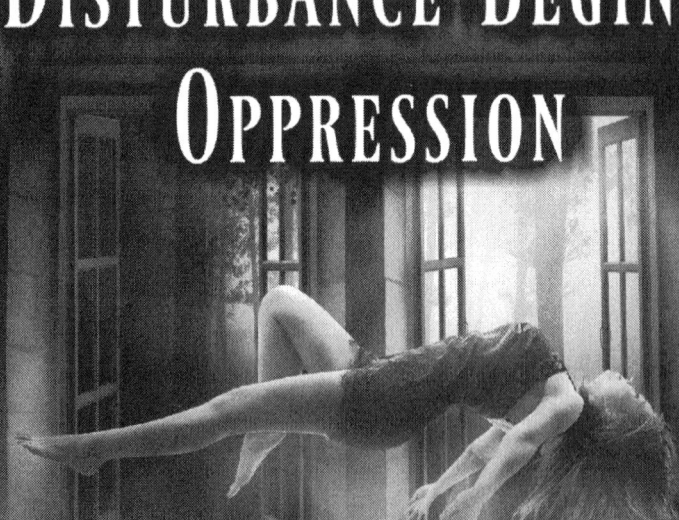

THE DARKNESS BEGINS

Now that one is in the awareness of how such entities can infest into one's life, it would suffice to say not much is surprising how they can intercept into the very depths of the home. My purpose is to enlighten one to the very core concepts and strategies to how these shadows can overtake your light by covering all hope in ever being released from the grip of despair. It is from this soul crumbling fate of the Demon or Familiar Spirit to take ahold of the living person's belief of freedom that remains to this day to be so successful. Demons have no concept of time, as discussed previously, and it's because of this universal factor that they are not limited to the time premise. With this truth, Demonic entities have an impressive amount of patience for humanity and will focus on one individual for most of their mortality. Waiting ever so quietly, so as to construct the perfect maneuvers for the human target to gain fear of their very existence at all. For the goal of the negative Spirit isn't just to create fear to the human target, but to encourage their belief that their very existence is cursed, mutilated, abolished, demented, unholy, tainted and something so unclean that even God won't come to save you.

THE UNHOLY TRINITY

It should be noted, that in order to properly identify an unclean, unfriendly Spirit, is to gain practice in noticing the entity's style to their haunting. Not all entities will haunt the living the same. For an example, a Demon haunting may appear as a little girl. The entity may try to attempt to lure the human target into a game of **Hide and Seek.** This is where the entity may begin to attempt to befriend the living target by making the person believe they are friendly, playful and may be simply lost. However, after being invested into the person's life, the entity will begin to unleash it's wrath with a venomous bite. Earth Bound Souls will arrive into a person's life differently however, for their agenda may not be equal to the Demonic nature. Human Spirits most often will approach a living human's home by acting out. The Earth Bound Spirit may begin to break objects, hit the living person and give them nightmares. But these fits won't be so orchestrated like the Demonic entity for the Demonic tend to form a carefully designed strategy that even an Earth Bound, nor a Familiar Spirit can convey. Familiar Spirits tend to behave rather odd for their traits may come as an unfamiliar characteristic.

Demon's play on the human emotions and psychological standpoint, where the human target is most susceptible. This focus alone is what creates an arena for mayhem with the unclean Spirit due to their ability to manipulate the living by playing on their deepest fears and even their most desired fantasies. This is played through what I call, ***The Unholy Trinity.*** The art of which the entity begins to play tricks on the living human victim by preforming Paranormal atrocities in a course, or pattern of three's. The three's pattern will consist of repetitive inexplicable annoyances and even disturbances within the home, or in your nightmares.

In the Christian religion, it's widely believed and adamantly taught the three's is the mockery of the Holy Trinity: *The Father, Son, and the Holy Spirit.*

This is true but only to a certain extent.

The Father, Son and the Holy Spirit connection may be suitable for the Christian believer, however from my journey as a Psychic Medium and as a Demonologist, I've encountered the understanding that the 'Father' isn't connected to the God concept, but to the Source, which is the higher power of love. The 'Son' concept isn't based on Jesus Christ, but on all people, that are children of love and creation in existence. Then finally, the 'Holy Spirit' is not to be based on God's Spirit or Spiritual presence in the world, but more so, based on the Spirit of all people that are of one energy within the course of the universe.

How one is to take this information isn't much of a priority for the understanding of this metaphorical connection doesn't necessarily matter when determining the lengths of your Paranormal haunting. No matter what one believes with the three's connection, is based on the individual respectfully, and isn't to be morally measured based one one's religious beliefs. It's best to remain humble that no matter how one determines this in their own interpretation, doesn't and won't change how the entity entered your life, nor how they leave. Religion isn't the Demon's nor the Familiar Spirit's agenda, nor is it their role in humanity. They're not limited nor are they restrained based on the script of religion, nor on the 'Damned' in other levels of dogma. They rely on your understanding of your ability to fight back -not on your level of interpretation. They're focus is on your conscious effort to remain fully aware of your very waves of thinking and appointed belief. For if they can have an open opportunity to trick your own moment of belief in *yourself* - that's the moment one's battle sets into motion.

THE PSYCHIC HOUR

You may come to discover the Paranormal Activity is intensified in the middle of the night. Commonly this may be called the *Psychic Hour*, or the *Witching Hour* for the time the activity heightens can be astronomical.

Considerably, entities are not bound by the earth time, however there is an energetic shift that occurs throughout the course of the cosmos that does correlate with earth's late hours. I honestly don't have a congruent answer for you as to why this is, but I do have several hypotheses to how these entities receive a higher level of energy. The first hypothesis is that because we are all made of energy, and because the universe is always in transition and transcendence, the energy reaches a higher level of intensity during certain moments of this circulation. It's a moment that seems to perhaps happen within a matter of minutes, but to us on earth it would seem as if a matter of hours when considering the time differences all around the world. But it's during these moments, the energy is at the highest level of power. When this shift occurs, the entities are then able to manipulate, or borrow this energy, in order to have a higher and more magnified impact for their activity.

The second hypothesis is based on the possibility, that when there is a considerable amount of people physically asleep at the same time, their psychic energy begins to take sizable impact on the energy around them. With this psychic energy raising during the moment a large amount of people are physically asleep, the negative spirits will drain those people's energy either by large quantities from a select few victims, or small increments from a massive population at one time.

Lastly, there's another possible currency for the entities to become stronger, and that is the moon taking the reins at night. This is not so unusual for those may experience a full dizzy spell during the course of a full moon. I for one experience this every full moon each month, along with undergoing numerous Astral Projection trips either before, or during a full moon. It's commonly believed and has been diligently traced back even to mythologies that the moon may carry some level of it's own psychic energy when at it a certain axis along the course of the day vs night. I'm no scientist, but I can attest, the moon has some level of energy that is especially dignified and differs from other planets, stars and even the sun.

As I've stated earlier, I don't claim to have all of the answers but regardless of why, or how this is, the entities are able to use this energy in order to continue their dirty work effectively.

THE PHANTOM'S LIST

For the sake of knowing what one should expect when in the dealings of a potential haunting, or of a Demonic terrorism, it's best to take a moment to study this portion. It's advisable to remain fully conscious of one's capability to measure the time the Paranormal activity occurs and how often.

To record effectively, one should also take a moment to notice how their initial emotions begin to feel. Feelings are a part of our *Divine Message Receiver*, which is in part of our intuition that allows the person to take heed on that initial gut feeling. It is in our intuition (psychic ability to discern) that which allows us with haste to respond to the situation based on the necessity or severity.

- Are you frightened?
- Are you curious?
- Are you nervous?
- Are you having an anxiety attack?
- Are you sweating?
- Are your hands and body shaking uncontrollably?
- Did you jump in fear?
- Did you retreat initially with terror?
- Were you calm?
- Were you fearless?
- Do you feel you need to sleep with a light on?

- Are you afraid of being alone?
- Are you suddenly fearful of the dark?

The list following is not to be measured based on least likely or most likely, for the consistency and expectancy of Paranormal Activity occurs individually based on the entity's desires. No Demon, human Earth Bound Spirit, or a Familiar will interact with the living the same as another, for they all possess their own level of intelligence and personalities.

Nightmares

If you find you wake up in a heap of fear, followed by a racing heart rate, you may have been *psychicly* attacked in your sleep. Take a moment to recall your nightmare. It's best to write them down during this time if you discover they happen often. These types of nightmares will be so lucid, you may find that you're literally staring at the Demon in the face. It's common for the targeted human to wake up from mild to severe bruising, scratches, burns, and even drained of energy after a Demonic nightmare.

These entities can put you into different dimensions, including the **Astral Realm** where they are able to manipulate and terrorize their victim most definitely. The *Astral Realm is a realm next after earth* which is the playground for how

Demons, Devils and even departed human souls can partake in Paranormal activity. The levels of other dimensions aren't so serious, for it's the Astral Realm and earth that are to be humanity's main concern.

Daymares

It's not unusual for a living person to be experiencing a lack of energy to the point where, out of the blue they may feel they need a nap. These moments will arrive as if you were suddenly hit with a tranquilizer gun. It will be so overwhelming, you'll practically start falling asleep instantly and may become dizzy. These naps are no accident, nor is it due to your body being low in nutrients, vitamins, etc. (Be sure to rule out any health concerns before ruling this as a Spiritual attack). What is to understand is these naps are forced upon the person in order to continue haunting, and hurting the person emotionally. It's cruel for their motive is to construct a strategic manner in order to force more emotional damage from these nightmares that happen during the day.

Shadow Figures

During a course of Paranormal activity, people most often report of seeing shadowy figures either standing in a hall, walking by them, or in the corner of their eye. These shadow figures are not loving, human souls. These are entities that crave on the negative aspect of energy, such as hatred, revenge, pain, fear, power, control, etc. Shadow figures can move up over your head onto the roof, or be as thick as a human being standing before you. The time of day to see these types of entities isn't limited. People have seen them during the early hours of the morning, to the darkest of nights. They can be transparent, or completely blackened to the point you cannot see anything through the figure. The level of thickness, weight, height, or shape doesn't and mustn't be assumed based on their abilities for as the old saying goes, 'don't judge a book by it's cover -or in this case, figure.

3's

There are a range of abilities and strategies that Demonic entities and even Familiars possess -and that's doing things in three's. This would include from bangs, knocks, taps, to even scratch marks in three's on the body. The three symbol is evidential for their intention is to mock the Holy Trinity (as discussed prior). Some have reported to having their phone ring three times but then to answer it to no one on the other line. Others have witnessed their doors open and close in a pattern of three times.

3 AM

During the highest level of energy, it's expected to become haunted by the time the clock reaches to 3 AM. Those that are undergoing an authentic Demonic attack may experience the worse portions of their Paranormal activity at the hours between 12 AM to 4 AM. This is due to the highest levels of Psychic energy as discussed before. When between these hours, the entity will be driven to begin having fun by dabbling within the home through the person's most vulnerable state after the person's guard has come down in order to relax and sleep. This allows the Demon to correspond with your emotions, and with the rest of the objects in the home. I've come to discover at this hour this is when their very presence is more susceptible to acknowledgement by your *intuition*.

Waking up at the exact hour of 3 AM is one of the most commonalities after having a nightmare. This is also the moment some may begin to examine the energy in the room and come to detect, sense, or feel a presence is there after the nightmare. The person may be frozen and frightened from this detection and not move from their original position, or out from their very bed for a long period of time.

Electromagnetic energy

This is one of the other potentials to experiencing Paranormal activity. Here the Demon or Familiar entity may acquire the energy in order to manipulate and startle those they are targeting by harnessing electricity from electronics such as cell phones, lights and even from storms. Light itself is an electromagnetic wave. It has been established through scientific studies to discover the connection to the speed of light and concluded that light is a form of electromagnetic radiation. It's also been established with EMF detectors, or (Electro Magnetic Field) detectors are used most often by Paranormal Investigators to detect a Spirit's presence for the known suspicion for Spirits to resonate with these same waves.

Health issues

When it comes to Demonic entities, they will make it their mission to get to the person emotionally, and mentally as much as possible. And one way to successfully do this is through the means of draining the person's health. Here the person may experience severe health complications, to even deterioration without a credible medical explanation. It is crucial for the person that may be undergoing these types of medical conditions, to be fully aware of their position. These entities don't just do these things to make you feel unhappy and miserable, for slowly but surely, it's a designed plan to prepare for your death in the end. If a person is being haunted for a long period of time by an entity like a Demon, the living person can be subject to being in this misery for up to forty years if the entity is able. Doing so is allowing them the availability to continue sucking your energy so they can continue to gain, while you slowly and painfully wilt away.

The person can begin to experience these types of health complications, leveled from being mild to the most severe. This brief list is not to be limited to only what is listed, and must be understood is something that should be carefully evaluated by your local doctor first, to make a concrete diagnosis. IF for any reason the doctors cannot find enough evidence to find the root of the cause of your medical situation, then that would be the moment to determine this as a psychic and spiritual attack.

- Severe headaches
- Dizziness
- Head pains (feelings as if someone is hitting you in the head or stabbing you with a sharp object)

- Unable to walk, sudden paralysis
- Severe nausea, vomiting (of food or blood)
- Blindness, blackouts
- Migraines
- Severe fainting spells
- Vertigo
- Numbness of certain parts of the body (must be ruled out from a medical physician before ruling it a spiritual attack)
- Heart attack(s)
- Stroke(s)
- Organ failure

Birds flock

While this may seem as a simple accident, the unfortunate truth is these entities can draw even birds to your home by forcing them to bash into a window and die. This may be witnessed when driving and a bird may collide with your vehicle killing the animal. There doesn't need to be large amounts of birds at a time for this to be considered a Spiritual sign, but must be again, noted as a potential, depending on the situation at hand along with other Paranormal experiences.

I know this for after my near-death experience my family's home would witness birds continue to crash and die into our windows several times in that year. These birds would die almost immediately upon impact which wasn't something we were accustomed to handling. Little did we know that this was a sign of a Demon in our midst.

Voices or Sounds

One may begin to hear unexplainable sounds, such as crashes, booms, or even a door slamming only to discover nothing of that sort occurred after investigating the noise. There's the commotion of those stating the fright of hearing voices that they cannot explain. Voices that may call their name, or say things in the distance, or even right up to the living person's ear or face. Once the person takes notice of this bizarre occurrence, unfortunately will be set with nothing to explain this strange phenomenon. Unexplained music has been heard by living people when in the motions of a series of Paranormal experiences. The sounds caused by an entity are not to be limited to only what is mentioned, for they're able to mimic voices of those you love, trust and of things that may attract or frighten you. A talent indeed, but a deadly one.

When in the moment of hearing this type of Paranormal phenomenon, it's best to remember where your emotions lie when initially triggered. Ask yourself what you're feeling. Remember to take a moment to feel what you sense from this moment when the activity is happening, so as to capture enough evidence to clarify the level of urgency. Even a voice as subtle as a little girl saying, "Hello there" can bring even the strongest man to his feet when caught off guard. No matter the type of voice one hears, is cautiously to maintain self-awareness at all times.

Physical Assault

Here is considered the highest potential of threat for once the entity that is haunting the person to resort of physical or sexual assault, is when your children and visitors of your home are also in danger. There are no limitations to the course of just how aggressive an entity can become when focused on hurting the living person(s). The range of being physically attacked can be as mild as a slight scratch on your arm, to the lengths of being pushed down a flight of stairs. There are countless reports of people experiencing physical attacks to even sexual assault. Below is a brief list:

- Being shoved or pushed.
- Being scratched.
- Finding Burns on your skin -while burning in the moment of discovery. The feeling of being burned is expressed as uncomfortably noticeable to unbearable.
- Being slapped by an unseen force.

- Hair pulled, tugged, or even ripped out from their scalp.
- Discovering a severe bruise without explanation.
- Being hit or punched by an unseen force accompanied by further bruising.
- Being pulled out of your bed at night during sleep.
- Awakening from sleep while experiencing the sensation of being choked, or suffocating without a logical explanation.
- Waking up from sleep with a force sitting heavily on top of you.
- Experiencing a disturbed sensation of being sexually assaulted while sleeping or in bed. May discover clothes have been misplaced, ripped off or torn.
- May experience being tripped without an explanation.
- May experience a door slamming, a cabinet, or any type of closing object on your fingers. Or the object may throw itself into you, giving a blow of pain or injury.
- May discover your hair or other body part suddenly catches fire without explanation.

Objects Moving

During Paranormal experiences, those may witness objects seeming to move, relocate or fly across the room inexplicably. This is somewhat rare, that is depending on the length and level of ability the entity is able to successfully do. Most often, it's a common misunderstanding that when an object moves, that it's the entity handling the object with their 'hands' or other body parts. This isn't the case for the entity is universal and isn't to be identified similar to a physical person that is living. What is happening, is the entity takes a great amount of focus with their psychic energy to manipulate that item by causing the object to move, giving the illusion of the entity handling the object. The entity isn't a physical body, so in order to handle things of matter, the entity must use heighted psychic abilities to maneuver objects causing them to float, open, close, fly, crash, dematerialize, or even hit you. During a legitimate Demonic haunting people have reported of their bed violently shaking in the middle of the night, or their windows breaking without an explanation.

I know this for I once had experienced an Astral Projection experience where I was met with my Master Spirit Guide and Twin Flame, allowing me the chance to witness this ability of Demons first hand. He allowed me this rare opportunity in order to witness this happening so as to explain how entities can do such things. The entity is not limited, and may become a physical apparition to handle a human that is living, but this would take the entity eons in order to achieve such a goal. The only force fully capable of this sort of act are the Devil beings that I know of *so far*.

Fly Infestation

Not too common will this occur, however sometimes during an authentic Demonic haunting there will be a commotion of flies in the home. These flies will usually be located in one part of the home, or work place, and will be followed with a cold chill in the room that is undeniable. Some have expressed during this infestation that they will get a sense of intense fear that *something* is watching them. The flies will most often be tested by an animal and insect expert such as an exterminator only to conclude that there is no evidence to support how, or why an infestation of flies is in the home.

Electronics

During the Infestation period of an unfriendly Spirit, it's commonly reported for individuals to experience their electronics act strangely. They may discover their cell phones shut off, turn on apps without explanation, or will find they begin to hear eerie noises during a phone call. It's odd yes, but entities have an ability to suck the energy from our electronic devices so as to catch our attention to spook us more. They may use the devices to regain further energy while burning out your lightbulbs, cell phone, computer, tablets, or even your television or radio. The moment these things occur, they will pay close attention to how you react to the situation. Those that may experience this may also feel in the moment that they are not permitted, or are being shut away from a specific person or situation. This is from the strong energetic impulses from the entity that will draw your emotions to these kinds of conclusions -that are not imaginary but *very* real. It's the entities goal to drive you mad with frustration, anger, and bring further emotional and mental stress to your wellbeing. If they find they can succeed by manipulating your electronics, they will continue to do so.

Those that are Lightworkers, Demonologists, Exorcists, or Psychic Mediums may find that when you're trying to do a project that is to bring further love and enlightenment -this will occur far too often. This is because the entity is trying to stop you from succeeding on your Lightwork mission. The entities targeting the person will experience a flood of negative psychic attacks such as their computer shutting off, freezing, or even finding it may just explode without explanation. Those in the work of Light will discover that they are dealing with their electronics continually malfunctioning, especially if they are driven to help people from negative forces.

Animals Acting Strange

You may come to find after waking up in the middle of the night that your pet is staring at something intensely that is not there. Or that your cat is hissing, or growling at a figure that doesn't seem to be visible. You may feel this immense fear in this moment followed by great concern. The pet during this difficult time may even shake, whimper, and hide in fear from this invisible force. Your beloved pet may shake so uncontrollably that they begin to urinate where they're positioned. If your cat becomes spooked they may find it necessary to jump on the roof, clawing at the doors in a hastened manner as if they're fighting to get away. The sign of our pets is crucial for animals possess a natural heightened sensitivity of energy due to their own Psychic abilities. The nature of animals is to be one with the course of their higher self at all times, for they're some of the purest forms of Spirits due to not being focused on the chaos of the world's issues. Granted, pets will become influenced by people's choices, however the innate courage of a pet is to follow their instincts initially without question. Following closely to how our pets behave, or any other animals around us, can be a helpful guide to the potential among us.

The unfortunate reality are the possibilities of discovering that your pet begins to have medical issues that seem to happen without warning. Some may say their pet suddenly couldn't walk, jump, or even eat normally. Once the owner were to take their pet to the Veterinarian, it's often decided after much educated analysis that the doctor cannot find a reason as to why the animal is struggling in this way. As unfair as it is, our precious pets may even be discovered lying lifeless with no explanation to how they suddenly died. Demonic entities will be able to influence their abilities and harm even those that we love the most, including our pets.

There seems to be a rumor that having a cat in your home will keep negative Spirits at bay. I can tell you with being raised with cats my whole life, it's never prevented nor scared of any Spirits or Demons. Demons are most certainly not fearful of cats.

Rotten aromas

The smell of rotten flesh or a dead carcass is most definitely to be expected when in the dealings of a Demonic, Familiar, and a Devil presence. The smell will be an exceptional potency when between the hours of 12 AM and 4 AM. The smell will usually be accompanied with Paranormal disturbances at this time due to the shared ugliness of the Demon's agenda. There are other aromas that can be followed through when being presented with a diabolical presence, such as, rotten eggs, rotten meat, or the smell of feces. These smells will be so strong that it could make the targeted living become sick from the very whiff in their nose. To be noted, the smell most likely will be within a certain location where the entity could very well be 'standing'.

In the year 2015, I was helping a person from a legitimate Demonic haunting. The person that I was trying to help expressed the same disturbances that I too began to undergo. For the purpose to scare me off from helping my client, the same entity began inflicting I and my young daughter with a series of terrorizing nightmares. These dreams would be so unbearable, I'd wake up screaming in utter fear. Not too long after these unprepared events, on a particular night I heard my daughter having similar nightmares, while screaming the word, "NO". As I rushed to her bedroom I had caught sight of the clock on our oven that said the time, 3:00 AM. Once I reached to her bedroom I was frozen in fear, for the moment I arrived to the hallway that lead to her bedroom door, there was a heart stricken doom that loomed within the atmosphere. Slowly I attempted to proceed with caution, however the closer I got the more I started to take in the smell of rotten eggs. As a Psychic Medium I've experienced this only a handful of times with a legitimate Demonic haunting, but in this moment, I was presented in the face of fear the reality that these entities took my work as a serious threat. Such a threat that they took it upon themselves to even target my own child. It was indeed a soul stricken awakening to just how merciless these beings can be.

Fires and Floods

As skeptical as this often is judged, there is nothing these entities won't attempt to see their goals accomplished. To go to the lengths of causing your pipes to burst, manifesting a flood to rush through the halls of your home. Or to turn all of your beloved memories to ash from a catastrophic fire explosion that is unexplainable even to specialists. Through these levels of chaos, preserves and nourishes the level of unsettling emotions the entities strive to produce so as to continue sucking energy from their victims.

Levitation

It's taught from Exorcists and other Demonologists that when a series of levitation occurrences happen, that its due to the moment a person becomes Possessed. This is true, but only to an extent however, for the victims don't have to be Possessed in the moment for objects to begin levitating in midair or the victims themselves. The purpose for the levitation is to produce extreme fear into the victim and witnesses. This type of fear is now personified by the very notion that there is no sense of control of the situation. This lack of control begins to produce an immense fear of the unknown which allows the Demon to become stronger in their ability. The course of levitation again, is similar to the ability when making objects move and even disappear. The difference however is in this moment, the objects being levitated aren't necessarily being moved to a location, but may also be hovered over their bed, lifted to the roof, or dropped back down. This motion is to inflict the person with an understanding that the Demon is now in control of the victim. It is in this particular moment, that enables the Demonic entity to engage in further fright and evidently most often succeed.

Finding Blood

Though being a rare occurrence, some have reported to discovering an obscene amount of feces, urine and even blood on the floor with no explanation to how, or why they got there. It may begin to occur either during the day or in the late hours, but there is no telling when the entity may produce these levels of filth. The logical approach is to quickly blame our pets (if we have any) when these unpleasant gifts arrive, however it would be best to carefully analyze the situation so as to be fair during this troubling time. It has also been reported for people taking a shower only to come out and find there are words written in blood on their bathroom mirror. Victims of Demonic

Oppression have equally shared the disturbing discoveries several times a day but may not even have a pet at all to properly explain these bizarre occurrences.

THE OPPRESSION OBSSESSION

It's inevitable that when a person is being victimized by these types of supernatural forces, there can become an addictive trait to seeing what can happen next. It's a tragedy, however I've come across a select few that claimed they wanted to be out of this terror, however were only feeding the fire more by admittingly taking part in openly communicating with the entities. This is where it can become nearly impossible to truly be rid of the Spirits once acknowledged by the living. Then they're granted the ability to continue their menacing ways without limitations further. It's true, that all they need to be more harmful is if the person willingly allows the entity to continue residing in their home or work place. During the Paranormal corruption the living person may find it in their heart to try to reason with the negative Spirits by asking them questions directing them in hopes of a morality or saving the Spirit. This is futile and must be accepted to never being able to reason with a force like a Demon. They are merciless and full of hatred so thick that not even the very God particle can change their consciousness -for they're a slave to their very existence.

After much deliberation, consideration from years of a thorough study, analysis and from experiencing my own terrors myself, these entities *want* you to be entertained. They want you to communicate with them, so to continue to strike back whenever they get the opportunity. These types of people that become easily addictive to the drama, to the chaos as a respected few, are considered easily susceptible to the negative influences.

If you find that you may have become attracted to this kind of Spiritual influence, it's not necessary to find blame or fault in the matter. This is what the entity wants, but if one were to discover this and address this within themselves openly, and quickly, then you'll be able to soon rescue yourself from their trance of erotic desire through chaos.

THE OPPRESSIVE CONFLICT AND PURSUIT

After weeks to even months of the Oppressive stage, the Demonic entity will have the emotional, and psychological grip on the victim. The victim is chosen through a careful analysis of their ability to fight back with their own will of stamina and own belief of self-worth. There are no other levels of reason to this madness, except to admit the person's possible inability to fight back. Not always will this be the case, for those being Oppressed by a negative entity can also be due to their innate connection to the Other Side, or their mission of Lightwork making them a possible threat. Those that are being Oppressed is to understand the psychological game these entities play onto the person that is being targeted, for the ultimate goal is to make the person fear that no matter what they do, no matter where they go, they aren't safe. This is a traumatic and a lonely place to be for within their mind, and in their heart, they begin to believe that not even God loves them enough to fight this terror back. They begin to feel that no matter where they are, that even when they are asleep they're prone to these Spiritual attackers.

This is what the Demon and Familiar's *want*. They want you to feel this way in order to maintain a dominance within your very mental compass. It is in this dangerous momentum that enables the Demon to further ravage and take hold of the person's very body, mind and even soul.

Chapter Eight

Influence and Possession

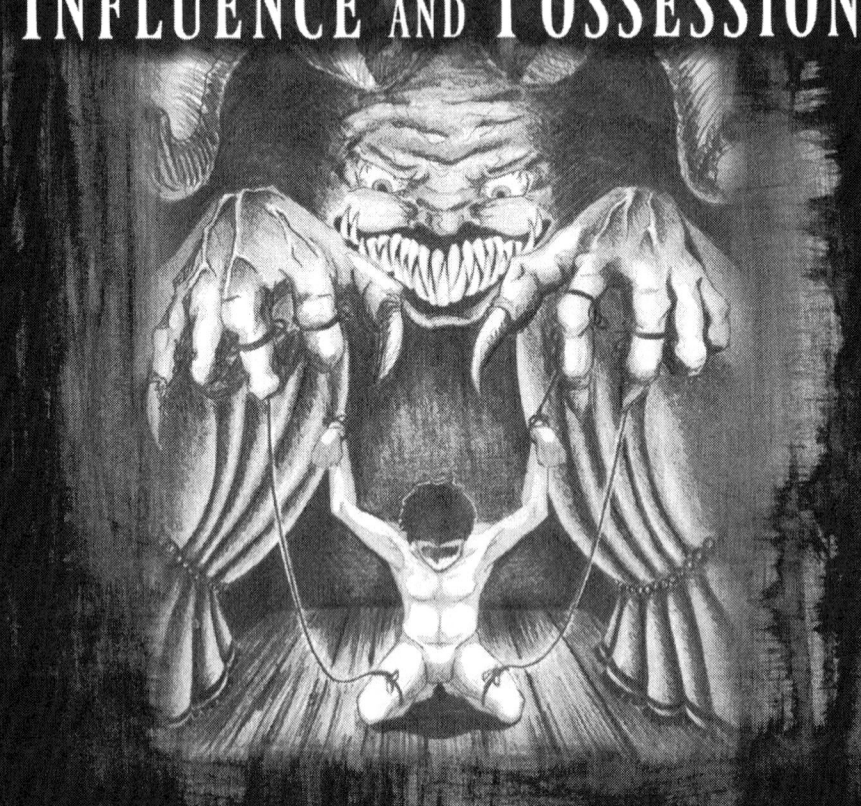

THE FOUR STAGES

There are several dynamics that go into play when a person is being Oppressed and is on the road to a possible Possession. I say, *possible* for the ability of the Demon or any entity to authentically Possess a living person is based on several key points. The key points are measured based on the agility and level of freedom the Demon has on the person. Depending on the power of influence the entity has on the living person is critical, for that amount of influence is what will determine the probability of the living person becoming the puppet of the metaphysical puppeteer.

When it comes to effectively determining the hold the entity has on the living target, it requires a person such as a Demonologist that understands these key points, in order to properly determine the victim's condition. It would be naïve, and frankly irresponsible to blankly state a person is currently Possessed without taking part in a series of tests to identify the genuine situation. For there are thousands of people a day that share they are feeling they are being *currently* Possessed, but this is faulty for the very concept of becoming genuinely Possessed is when the living person is *no longer in charge of their very brain, and body.* The person that would be Possessed wouldn't even be able to state they are concerned with *being* Possessed -however this doesn't insinuate the person may not be still facing a real life threatening Spiritual warfare.

Before the stage of Possession occurs, there is what I have identified as the **Influence** stage. Though it's commonly taught of there only being three stages of a genuine Demonic haunting, I've discovered after careful examinations from my own Demonic encounters with countless clients, that there are in fact **four stages** to this diabolical battle. To cover each step by step, to better understand the mind and strategy of a malicious entity, I would like to remind you what these stages are, and why they are so effective:

STAGE ONE: INFESTATION

This is where the entity is given the chance to infest into your life or others. Here the entity may become summoned, conjured, or simply where the person is at the wrong place, at the wrong time. Or if the person recently *awakened* and has become a new potential target.

STAGE TWO: OPPRESSION

Here is when the entity begins the Paranormal horror on the family within the household. This is the time where the entity makes their presence known through expressing their power and desire for control, by implanting the emotion of fear. It is the entity's goal to get the victims to feel hopeless, helpless, and to give in with their free will by believing there is nothing left to keep them safe. This is the moment where the entity will focus most of their energy onto one specific person, (sometimes two people) after determining the person's possible inability to fight back. *This is one of the main reasons to why Demonic entities will often choose children.*

STAGE THREE: INFLUENCE
(COMMONLY MISSED DIAGNOSIS)

This is the stage most Demonologists and even trained Exorcists **miss**. This is where the entity begins to negatively influence the person by motioning the person desires and behaviors they wouldn't normally partake willingly. This isn't Possession *yet,* due to the living person still having a hold on their free will to choose these sorts of reactions and behaviors. In the stage of Influence the entity begins to encourage the living person to do things, say things that wouldn't be their true character. However, during this time the Demon doesn't have a full hold on the living targeted person because this only happens in moments. Here the entity will influence the person in certain moments from their attitude, which is an emotional, mental, and truly psychological game they can play for months if they choose. The negative Influence can take the entity weeks to successfully engage in with the living person, and the living person will most often be completely unaware that this is happening at all. Because the entity isn't fully immersed into the living person's mental capacity yet, it's one of the most common stages that are regretfully overlooked -which is the stage that can be ***stopped*** before the moment of a true Possession occurs.

STAGE FOUR: POSSESSION

This is the final and most deadly stage a person can go. Here this is the moment the living person has willfully given into the fight of this Spiritual battle which allows the entity to now move into their physical capacity. The person will no longer have much power over their mind and body and will engage into traits and behaviors that will be unsettling to those witnessing the Possessive person. Those that are genuinely Possessed will require a great deal of help from a *higher* power in order to fully be free from the chains of a supernatural slavery. Possession can begin to happen as soon as within a few weeks after a Demon begins to haunt the targeted individuals. However, that is only based on the amount of lack of will to remain dominant within the situation. If a person isn't easily accessible, the Demon will likely decide to construct a course of possible strategies that could take the entity weeks, months, to even years to successfully Possess the person. Although this would seem to be a waste of time to us, the entities are not limited nor are they bound by earth time. It's fair to say the idea of waiting a few years isn't much, nor may it be a negative aspect to them in the slightest.

THE INFLUENCE TEST

During the stage of Influence, it is considerably inherent for those being Influenced to overlook the severity to their behaviors and changes in mental health. It's a commonality through those being Influenced to feel this may be their fault for not seeing the signs in advance, nor being able to have a better hold on their own choices or reactions. Although there will be things the Influenced person may commit, doesn't mean they should be put to fault or shamed over their chosen actions or reactions. For its in the Demon's discourtesy to engage the person in a series of mannerisms that wouldn't be suitable to those of even the least civilized. The power of the Demon's Influence can be measured based on how the person's anger arises during certain situations or dilemmas. Not all Influenced individuals will react, or act the same way. To better analyze the situation based on the individual's personality and past chosen behavior and character traits -is to begin comparing the potential influenced person's behaviors to their behaviors prior to the influential condition.

For example, If the person that is allegedly being Influenced by a negative Spirit, the person may begin to have sudden outbursts of rage and may physically begin striking other people in the home. However, maybe a few months ago, the living person was an anti-violence believer, never agreeing or supporting this kind of abuse.

To better examine all areas of the allegedly Influenced living person (or yourself) is to take a moment to read the follow behavioral changes that may be happening currently, or in the past few weeks. These traits and behaviors are more so a change in personality, not based on the person's loss of free will. These changes would be when the person suddenly 'decides' on their own to behave or act a certain way. Most of these Influenced moments are brief, and won't last for very long -which is why most often this is so easily overlooked by professionals in the field.

- The Influenced person may experience sudden outbursts of rage and animosity towards others or a current situation. This moment of anger will only last for a few minutes IF the person is able to shake this by regaining full awareness of themselves. Or the person seems to be having outburst several times a day without any medical or logical reason as to why.

- The person being Influenced may start a series of harmful acts towards themselves, or others. Some that are severely Influenced can begin to become serial killers, child molesters, abusers, murderers people and of animals, to a rapist. These are a specific kind of Influence, for the person may already have some level of apathy already. With this lack of empathy, the person can become easier to influence by the entity encouraging the person to commit such terrible crimes.

- The Influenced person may struggle with getting a full night's rest. May wake up feeling weak with a severe amount of fatigue, even after having over six hours of sleep the previous night.

- The Influenced person may experience nightmares or daymares.

- The Influenced person may begin to be easily irritated and severely impatient with people and situations.

- The person undergoing a Demonic influence may experience moments of staring off into space. This is where the person seems to lose a concept of time, but is to be understood, is only a slight loss of focus. Not always will this be rooted to a negative Influence, but if this were to happen during moments when the person is in the middle of doing something, this can indicate a Spiritual Influence.

- Does the person suddenly have a lack of empathy for others?

- There may be times where the person is suddenly odd in their personality. They may mumble to themselves, or say things that seem random and irrational for a moment. This would have to be completely out of the person's character.

- The person being Influenced would experience moments of sleep walking, or sleep talking. This would have to be something that begins to happen often. It would be required to be noted on how many times this happens per night and what is being said by the person during their sleep walk. This will happen when a person that is a *sensitive* to Spiritual energies to behave this way in new locations, such as hotels or homes they're visiting. It's carefully outlined that this can happen most often in children for their unable to be aware of exactly what is Influencing them.

- Does the person suddenly not care to be in public places or spend time with family, or friends? A person becoming a sudden recluse is essential for the entity to take a greater hold on the person that is targeted, which is why this is a crucial key component to a successful Possession. However, if the person was always considered a recluse, it's not substantial enough to insinuate Influence stage.

If you've answered *yes* to most of these key points of potential Influence signs, then it would be unfortunate to suggest that **_now_** would be the time to seek immediate Spiritual Counsel from an experienced individual in Demonology.

GENUINE POSSESSION VS TV POSSESSION

It's not a mystery that most people follow to the word Possession with the ideology of the person becoming like that of a monster. This is true. The entity begins to take a hold of the person in a sense that is damaging to the person's very dignity of their very existence, however what one witnesses commonly on television isn't always going to be the case. Comparing what one most often expects in a Possession are extravagant emotional explosions, even to the point where they may witness magical moments occur among the room where the Possessed person resides. They may encounter the Possessed begin to twist their body in a way where the very bones begin to break of the living person, which is true, but is exceptionally rare. Some may expect from the power of television to be witnessing the possessed person to become like that of a powerhouse of energy, and even levitate in midair while condemning others in the room to a hellish experience. However, this isn't always the case. A genuinely Possessed person won't always engage in this manner. To include, it's considerably rare if a person actually levitates during a Possession or during the moment they are being Exorcised. Can this happen? YES. But will it always happen? No, for it depends on the power and determination of the Demon(s) that are Possessing the person.

GENUINE POSSESSION SIGNS

In order to properly identify a genuine Possession case, is to take note of certain behavioral trait alterations that can occur during the course of the final two stages. The final stages, Influence and Possession are significantly heightened in the means of danger for the person won't be solely faced with a physical threat, but of the means of psychological damage. The person that is being Possessed isn't fighting against regaining the reins of their body, but of their soul's capability to withstand the mental game these pranksters and Spiritual monsters play. The entity will then have the momentum to take full control of the living person by overrunning the living person through a soulful corruption.

Below is a list of what to expect when a person is genuinely Possessed, but to remain aware that not all signs are going to appear during someone's Possessive state. Not always will everything occur that one would fear due the reality that Demons have their own personalities and will Possess a person in their own way.

SUDDEN OUTBURST OF RAGE

Here the person that is being Possessed will begin to have sudden outburst of rage that will be seemingly out of character of the person. Their rage will be so vile they may begin to throw things, break things unexpectedly with no logic nor reason. The individual may also begin to swear if they weren't one to use fowl language prior. During the course of the outburst, the people witnessing this behavior may experience a feeling of extreme fear from the Possessed person. The fear will feel as if their loved ones don't 'know' this person anymore or at all. These outburst of rage can happen over the most minimal of situations that will enrage the person so much, that they may strike those they love, including children. This can also occur when the person is under the influence of drugs or alcohol.

Hate Towards Religion or Love

Those that undergo a genuine Possession will experience a range of disturbed emotions. One including an insatiable hate towards religious icons such as nuns, preachers, pastors, and priests. This also includes those of a loving nature that are residing on a positive energy field with pure intentions. This hate will be exceedingly overwhelming for they may begin screaming violently, following the course of striking anyone in their way. The Possessed person will take a great distain for locations such as a church, due to the course of church being a place of positive vibes such as love, forgiveness, mercy, and goodness. It would not be so unusual for the Possessed to spit, smack, or kick those of a religious path. Some have reported to even seeing the Possessed person attempting to murder those of this belief for the sake of utter hatred. The Demon's nature is the exact opposite which would explain this insurmountable disgust.

Those under the grips of a Possession may also show aggression towards religions items like a cross or other religious trinkets that encourage positive vibrations. Some have reported for a Possessed person's skin to begin burning if they were to hold a cross in hand or having it pressed against their skin.

Sleep Walking

It is to be expected for a person that is experiencing a Possessive state, to begin having sleep walking episodes. Those experiencing the sleep walking may not even be fully aware that they are doing it. Sometimes the person may awaken during sleep walking occurring. This can be life altering and chilling to the person for they'll be standing in the dark wondering how they got there. Sleep walking can happen several times in a week, and even during naps that are taken in the daytime. At times the person sleep walking may also discover severe bruising, or even falling down the stairs. It's especially serious when this occurs, for this is the moment the person that is being targeted is already in the process of temporarily being physically Possessed. This can be life threatening due to the amount of dangers the person can get into during their sleep walking episode. The Possessed person could very well be sleep walking while being lead out of their house and into a road where a car can hit the person. If sleep walking begins to occur *(even during the Influence Stage),* this is when the person is in real danger and mustn't be overlooked.

Speech Changes

If the person begins to speak in tongues, such as in different languages, or accents then this would be something to pay close attention to. If you were to take an old record player and play the song backwards, you will hear the words spoken in reverse, this would also be a probability when dealing with a possible Possession. The very tone of the voice coming from the person may fluctuate. The pitch could descend as deep as a grown man, yet the person Possessed may be a young girl or boy. These vocal changes can happen at anytime, but will become more prominent when the person Possessed is experiencing explosive episodes.

Facial Changes

Here the individual may alter in their physical appearance, so much to the point it may be shocking to others witnessing the Possession. They may be so unrecognizable especially in the nose, eyes, eye brows and cheeks. This is due to the entity that is Possessing the victim beginning to overtake their physical appearance. Within the deepest parts of the soul tends to be seen through the eyes of the person, which is why when looking directly at those Possessed may develop extreme discomfort. Even if the person that is Possessed is a five year old girl, the parents will struggle with seeing their child in this diabolical state. A soul shaking reality that it's no longer their child in control of this tiny body that was once their precious offspring.

Smells Permeating

An overwhelming less than pleasant aroma may permeate from the person that is undergoing a genuine Possession. It's the overbearing smell of rotten flesh, garbage, urine, feces or other bodily fluids. The person being Possessed won't even notice this aroma that has now become their norm. It's to be credited, that the person Possessed isn't responsible for these smells most often, but are due to the entity beginning to engage in exposing it's truest form that it embodies.

Sudden Psychic Powers

Within the course of a Possession the individual shall exert an exceptional ability in reading people's past, predicting the future, and the present. As previously stated, Demonic and Familiar Spirits will have excelled powers through the use of their Psychic Abilities. The Demon will be able to read all situations, fears, doubts, thoughts, and deepest desires that may seem shameful to those witnessing. During this point the entity may attempt to embarrass those present by laying out all of the information they've collected and use it mercilessly. Those engaging with the person that is Possessed must remain aware that this is not the person you love anymore, this is the Demon(s) talking.

Super human strength

When the entity that is Possessing the person feels threatened or wants to show who's boss, will explode with intense super human strength. So overpowering, that it could overthrow the room as if there were four grown men shaping and managing the body of the Possessed victim. The Demon is a supernatural fugitive and will stop at nothing to show where they stand either within the body or within the very room. No person should take it upon themselves to handle the Possessed victim alone, for it wouldn't take much effort for the Possessed to harm those they love. Those within the Possessive state will have the ability to throw people across a room, chairs, and even large pieces of furniture. Not one person is immune to the wrath of the Demonic entity and nor would it be wise to assume so.

Levitation

In the case of a genuine Possession the person(s) involved and, including the one being Possessed, may experience a mystical fear of levitation. The levitation experience may seem like a lucid dream at first if discovered in the middle of the night while the Possessed person is asleep. However, there may come a time where the levitation can quickly turn into a human's horror. The person levitating could be thrown to the roof of the home, to the walls, or may become involved in a levitation disarray where they don't seem to reach the ground for a long period of time. The levitation is a part of the entity's Psychokinetic Ability as discussed previously.

Personality changes

If the person develops a sudden apathy for sentient life, then this could become a potential future threat. The individual that may be Possessed may not extend a hand of empathy, nor care, or concern for those around them the way they used to. This is a character alteration that must be carefully analyzed without the Possessed person being made aware. As the person may have smiled often, and laughed, the person that is being Possessed may sway from those basic human joys by no longer smiling, no longer laughing, and may not even express any type of human emotion at all. The person could mumble to themselves in the dark, begin writing words or saying things that don't seem to make sense, can also be a sign. Those that are Possessed may be caught scratching the floors or the walls as if like that of an animal. They could do this for so many hours that they begin to make their nails rip off and bleed. Their behavior could resort to scratching their head in one spot so often that their hair begins to fall out or is being ripped from the scalp. They may even begin to bang their head aggressively against a wall or ground.

*There are emotional, and mental disabilities that must be ruled out *first* from a trained, clinical physician before resorting to this as a Spiritual attack. Must also rule out drugs, and alcohol usage history -however, that doesn't suddenly dispel the probability of a genuine Possessive Stage.

Fascination of harm

In the event the person starts to self-harm, or if they become fascinated with knives, scissors, guns, or other dangerous objects/ weapons, then this would be something to be weary over. Especially if the individual is suddenly fancied toward the concept of revenge or with the idea of death, killing people or animals -then this is the time to be ***extremely concerned.*** These warning signs can be subtle but if carefully examined in all areas of emotional, social, and mental capacities it may pop out like a giant red flag. If addressed as soon as possible then the potential threat can be prevented if caught early.

Burns and scratches

During the stage of Possession, the person that is being Spiritually harnessed by the clutches of Demons, may be submerged in the indulgence of burns and cuts. These burns will set off even flames onto the person that which causes their very skin to smell of burning flesh. There is an availability for the entity to begin even scratching and cutting the person's body either from within the body's interior or on the exterior. There are no limits to how the entity will engage in physically mutilating the person's body. Some that witness those being Possessed may express the individual's body begins to smoke as if their very body was on fire. Some say this is due to the entity's entrance being from the pits of Hell. I don't have that answer. But what I do sense, it's simply possible the agony of being burned alive would suffice the Demons further enjoyment of watching them suffer.

Teleportation

In the events of a person being personally victimized by a Demonic Spirit, may experience moments where they are suddenly somewhere else without a logical explanation. It's evident for the person to be aware of what they were doing before the moment the teleportation occurred. In this ability, the entity is able to manipulate the victim's surroundings, emotional stamina and arrange a menacing stance onto the person. Teleportation can occur when the person is either asleep or awake. When the teleporting moment arises, it's best to try to find the person as soon as possible if you were a witness to this Psychic attack. There is not much that can be done to prevent a teleportation episode. However, the person can be pinned onto a bed for a temporary time with people watching over him/her, or with the use of restraints, while the Possessed person is closely observed.

Trance Episodes

It should be made aware that those being targeted by a negative influence like a Demonic entity, may become entranced so deep to the point they seem unresponsive. This will occur at what seems random moments. The person being in this deep trance may either go willingly into the trance or can be pulled into it unwillingly. There should be no fault presented during these occurrences for the Psychic pull to be engaged in the trance is exceptionally overpowering even to the most skilled of Psychics and Mediums. During the trance the person that is in the trance may begin to speak to someone that the witnesses of the trance don't physically see. The trance experience is not to be taken lightly as like a manifested dream, for this is another form of a Psychic attack where the entity Spiritually kidnaps the person's conscience and places them into another dimension that is beyond physical matter. A person that is being attacked while being engaged in the trance can physically become harmed. If the person is cut or burned in the trance, then so can their physical embodiment. This is a battle through the use of Psychic energy and would require a highly trained Psychic, or Demonologists, followed with prayer to rescue the person.

However sometimes, there's also to be noted that there may be experiences that may seem so lucid to the person in the trance, but to reassure that those experiences are most often illusions brought on by the Demonic Spirit. So, to say, the person can become physically harmed during the trance, but sometimes they won't and it's just another scare tactic. Ultimately, it depends on the choice of the entity.

Creepy crawly

The individual that is being Possessed by a negative Spirit may be enticed with the human body and engage the person's body in a series of strange happenings. The entity could start to crawl what seems like an upside down motion that would normally be difficult for the living person. But when doing so, this may be exceedingly easy for the entity that is Possessing the person. Their bones may start dislocating as if on purpose in order for the Demon to make a home into the person's body. The purpose of this is to dehumanize the person that is being targeted. It's very nature is to desolate the human's residence within the concept of their own temporary temple where the soul rests.

SEVERE HEALTH DEPLETION

A depletion in health can be a sure sign of the person that is experiencing the Possession stage. In this case the person that's targeted will experience a lack of energy, and will wear a grave look upon their face. They may look as if they are the walking dead for the purpose of the entity is sucking the energy out of the person incredibly. Their expression will seem as if they're out of the desire for life, and may even struggle with finding energy to get out of bed at times. The entity that is sucking their energy can very well be so attached to the person that no matter how many hours they sleep, they never seem to have enough energy.

THE SPIRITUAL REALITY

It's a distasteful inferiority that those within the depths of the Demon's endurance will become a slave to the body they were once in control of. The likelihood of multiple Demon's taking a hold on one person is not as common, for the very capability for Demon's to partake into this position must be exceptionally able to construct the person into the right kind of Spiritual bondage. However, there are millions of Demonic entities, so the possibility of this occurring is still a considerable reality that should be taken seriously. Some

Demonic Possessions have been reported to having to expel as many as over sixty entities from one Possessed person, however this is exceptionally rare. Most often there will be multiple entities, but not nearly as many for it would depend on the ultimate goal of the entities, and the orders from the Descended Masters -Devils.

It's commonly taught throughout the United States and parts of Europe that those that become targeted by Demonic forces is due to lack of faith in God or a religion. This is a down right **myth.** There is no relevance to the lack of faith, for even those that are exceedingly faithful in their religion, or belief of choice, are still capable and have indeed become a target. The person's choice of faith has no foundation nor a connection to the Demonic Infestation, Oppression, Influence, or Possession. It's a sure disappointment to teach this for then it encourages shame and places fault on the person that is being targeted. This is not the case, and shouldn't be proclaimed so loosely, for the dynamic of how and why a Demon enters and terrorizes a person's life is increasingly complex. There is no room to place fault based on one's religion, faith, or lack thereof.

It would be wise to reminisce on the history of religion that initiated the blame game, so as to reinstate the religious motive in order to convert future members. A medieval concept, fearful of free thinking that enabled the church further power to conquer those of other beliefs, and walks of life. Neither bias, however the motive from those of this belief corrupted countless styles of free-thinking, which would explain the motion to point the finger at the victim so harshly to this *very day*. I should know, I've experienced this blame game for years and the blame continues on, like the stream of this barbaric teaching.

In addition, the equally disturbed lessons within the faith of Christianity and other similar religions, that it's due to the person's *sinful* lifestyle choices that caused the Demonic attacks. Again, another **myth that must be debunked with full force.**

Demons don't care about your lifestyle choices, they care about the ability to withstand the spiritual warfare of all things. Their very target is measured on the capability to become Influenced by a range of potentialities, and based on your growing up. If you were a person that was abused as a child, then the Demon will target the person with that type of history by feeding the person with the idea that they are loved and cared for by this entity. The Demon may extend their help by providing revenge on those that hurt them, giving the living person a sense of support and attention they perhaps were neglected of as a child. These entities perverse their way into the person's life through their will and deepest desires that even the person may not be fully conscious of. There is no sense, nor is it compassionate to put full blame onto those that undergo these types of Spiritual attacks. Nor should there be guilt harvested upon the shoulders of yourself if you've been victimized and allowed them into your life. There is no reason to resort to self-blame. If you were indeed tricked by the ultimate trickster, for the very motivation of these walking shadows is to permeate your aura with a sense of shame and guilt, to further contaminate your higher sense of self.

However, it's to be clear, there are those that willingly conjure Demons for their bidding so carelessly. It's a heart-stricken reality I was faced to remember -yesterday, in fact. For there are those that willfully choose to work closely with these menacing conjured beings for the sake of their vanity, ego, selfish desires, greed, and even revenge by requesting death to come onto their enemies. What's worse, is these wishes do come *true* -but always at a *karmic price.*

Chapter Nine

The Ultimate Power to Freedom

THE POWER FROM WITHIN

There is no such thing as a coincidence, for today as I begin to write this portion, I was motioned by my Spirit Guides, to take note of the date on my computer, and come to find today is, 11/1/2017. In case you weren't aware, the number 1 in numerology is quite powerful for this encourages one to remain aware of their inner wisdom and ascended guidance from Angels. When you look at the date, the numbers 111 are in place first at this very moment I write this portion for you. Here it is to signify the powerful number of *manifesting* and *manifestation*. Which is to encourage the deep rooted cosmic understanding that one cannot succeed to what one cannot truly believe. Without the inner belief of one being able to find true peace from the poignant collide of pure hatred, there is no hope.

Naturally, one would assume that this last bit of guidance would be to presume it would be to find an Exorcist, in order to alleviate the diabolic trademark of fear and control. However, that's only a small portion to the truth of how one is truly free from Demon's and Familiars. As helpful as an Exorcist would be, it will only do so much, for the true power of release comes from the person's soul willingly letting go of the clutches of these dark forces and fighting back to their light. It's inevitable to seek Spiritual counsel from those that are most aware of their cosmic energy, however even the most sought after Exorcists, or Spiritual catalyst cannot save you from the

Spiritual warfare fully. For what isn't taught in religion, nor in your local church is the Spiritual battle is something being done from within your consciousness. A Spiritual warfare that is most definitely real and repulsive, but can *only* be completely released when the person that is being Possessed discovers within themselves the power of *light* and *love*.

THE EXORCISM AND EXORCIST

The moment one is in dire need of an Exorcist is when the person is truly incapable of conquering the battle themselves, and, or feel this is the road most comfortable for them. Not all Possessive states will require a full Exorcism for it depends upon the threat of the battle itself. For there are two kinds of Exorcisms, an **Exorcism of the person** that is being Possessed, or an **Exorcism of the location** where the entity resides. In order to achieve the right kind of Exorcism, requires the right kind of individuals to articulate what those needs are after a careful examination of the situation. One cannot simply look and diagnose the issue, one must take time to carefully analyze the dilemma with an innate *intuition* that is guided by love for all concerned.

As contemporary as my teachings may appear, there is indeed a rise of those becoming Demonically Influenced and Possessed. It's been reported of a disturbing increase in the number of Exorcisms performed between the early 1960's and 1970's. Thousands of potential victims' families take it upon themselves to reach out to those of the church in hopes to seek refuge and be freed from the Devilish grasp. However, as many of those thousands of letters are sent, so do many of them become, yet another unanswered prayer.

The reason for this is not the fault of the church nor of any religious group, but for the fact that most people don't realize you can still seek help from many other types of Spiritual Counsel. Because the Catholic faith and Christianity have become considerably overwhelmed with taking it upon their own to fight this cosmic battle alone. And because of this, there is a limited amount of leverage in answering all those that seek help. Due to this outdated dominance, those in these faiths are becoming rapidly outnumbered. It is to be reminded that there's plenty of other Spiritual Counsels out there to help alongside them. The right kind of Spiritual Counsel depends on you and those in care of the person that is being Demonically targeted.

SPIRITUAL NOTE

If you feel that a person you know is Demonically Possessed after reading, then it would be suggested to seek immediate counsel as soon as possible. Those of any level of Spiritual Counsel most often have a handful of experts in this sort of battle and would be best to notify immediately. Being that I'm not an Exorcist, I would highly recommend someone that you can contact that is experienced in this Spiritual Oppression in order to acquire the help of your loved one. Those that are genuinely Possessed will not usually remotely suspect that they are Possessed, for this is an exceptionally well organized, and Psychicly skilled attack that even the most impressive of

Psychics, Demonologists and Priests can overlook even within themselves.

THE UNFORTUNATE TRUTH

As a Demonologist, I've encountered only a few cases where the person being targeted by a Demonic force was credible. However, each case must be taken seriously regardless of these odds for the person being at risk is still a reality. Through these experiences however, I've come to the disappointing conclusion that most often people are turned down by those that seek refuge from their Church. For once I was appointed by a client named, "Jessica" *(name changed for discretion)* and her family were being haunted by three Demonic forces at once. And although her evidence was founded and acknowledged, the Priest that arrived at her house didn't know what to do. Unbeknownst to my client, the Church sent a Priest that was still in training. He had no knowledge, nor any kind of experience in the field. The young man must've been no older than his mid-twenties. Only being there for a few minutes, "Jessica" expressed to him of her greatest concerns. Sharing with him photographs of the entities in her closet, along with him hearing the entities voices on a voice recorder, that my client took time to preform for her own sake of gathering evidence. The naïve Priest was sweating, she said. He took mere glances in certain locations, and was beginning to get dizzy. Yet after only a few moments in her home, the inexperienced Priest fearfully fled her residence, telling my client he didn't have an answer for her. A few weeks later, "Jessica" received a letter written from the head Priest of her Church, instructing her that the reason for their disposal of their services was due to her own doing. The Church told her that there was nothing they could do for her. Instructing in the letter that the only person she could blame was herself for only those that aren't truly faithful in Jesus Christ were solely responsible.

Distraught and feeling overly defeated, "Jessica" helplessly wrote to another Church and religious official online, in hopes that if she could reach to someone out of her state, then perhaps this would allow her a chance at freedom. "Jessica" pleaded for help from this person, asking for any answer that could allow her and her family guidance. However, to no avail, the same answer came in the form of a text message. Being that she had internet on her phone, "Jessica" was kind enough to present me with feedback of this letter, here the letter is shared as it was written:

"The first thing that needs to happen is finding a faith community to pray with on a regular basis. Catholic or Protestant, whatever your faith background is, just make sure the community is upbeat and not prone to angry or hateful rhetoric. These spiritual challenges are not fixed by an exorcism, that is reserved only for the possessed. When one is obsessed or vexed, that is when someone believes the Demonic are trying to disrupt their life, then it also is a matter of faith. Prayer and faith come from an interior decision to attend church, read scripture, and pray. No one person has the power to do this for someone

else. This is a decision and faith practice. Exorcism is used in cases of possession and follows a period of discernment with the pastor or priest that you work with, a medical exam, and a comprehensive psychological screening. This is not optional; it is a vital part of the whole process. We do not believe that the concept of generational curse is a reality. Every person has the right to choose their own faith life, nothing removes our free will. Baptism is the rebirth of a child, or adult in the Christian faith. To believe in generational curses is to deny the power of that sacrament. If you have not been baptized it would be prudent to do so, after a period of study and prayer so that the desire is truly present, not as a quick fix. "
Sincerely, (name left anonymous)
Executive Assistant to the Exorcist of the Archdiocese of Indianapolis

After receiving this defeating setback in getting help, that's when "Jessica" discovered me through my YouTube channel and contacted me with sincere desperation. When I took a few hours to fully examine "Jessica's" case, she was indeed over her head, and so I took a few days to carefully analyze all areas of her living and wellbeing.

Not being a psychologist, I took a few hours with her so as to examine her mentality, and her intentions based on the situation. Within a few minutes of our conversation it was clear to me this woman wasn't under the influence of drugs, alcohol, nor was she seeming to be in the hindrance of a mental or psychological diagnosis. "Jessica" was more than forthcoming, expressing her homework on the Paranormal, and even going to the lengths of telling me that she was seeing a therapist in the past for other concerns but was not diagnosed with anything that could relate to her situation. Granted, I'm not a doctor, but as an advanced Psychic Medium I've developed a certain skill in being able to determine when a person is lying, or is not being as forthcoming. The closer I got to where she was emotionally and mentally, I did come to uncover the unsettling truth that she was indeed becoming obsessed with the drama of Paranormal conflict -but she was indeed being terrorized by three Demonic forces.

The conclusion arrived just before I had our session over the phone, for "Jessica" lives in another state from I. Being that our session was only to be over the phone, I had absolutely no knowledge of her living, nor of her exact situation in the moment when I scheduled for her session.

When I schedule clients that are concerned with Paranormal Activity, I help these clients completely free of charge, for I believe that it's not a person's fault, and shouldn't have to pay for something they rightfully didn't ask for. With that being said, I took it upon myself to heed her calling by taking nearly three weeks to slowly uncover what she was dealing with.

However, as a Psychic Medium the common shell shocking turbulence that a person may be undergoing in their home, will begin to start happening in mine. And that's just what occurred. The three Demons haunting "Jessica's" family began to haunt and terrorize myself along with my young daughter. I began to have nightmares followed with discovering bruises on my body that I could not explain. Banging would begin to occur just over or next to my head in the late hours of the night, or a series of loud scratching noises as if something was scratching up the walls of my bedroom. I'd experience something pulling my leg that nearly dragged me out of my bed when asleep, along with having a vision of the very entity haunting her family that I'd never forget.

When I receive these types of Psychic visions, they're extremely vivid. This vision was so lucid that the moment I closed my eyes, I went into a deep trance that I didn't intentionally volunteer. Once I got into a certain point of the trance, that's when I saw the entity's face staring back at me. I could make out all of it's grotesque details. From it's eyes, ears, chin, all the way to it's hair follicles. But what took most of my attention was the long nose positioned on it's face that was supported by a seemingly creepy grin. Within a few seconds being in this trance, wishing I could get out of it, that's when the entity spoke to me saying, *"Now,.. you see me."* During the trance I had heard it's voice within the Psychic communication through Telepathy. The energetic vibration of the entity was close to intolerable, but it was in this experience that I was able to further help my client.

It wasn't until that moment after I awoke from the trance that I knew "Jessica" was telling the truth and was indeed in a heap of danger. Once we had our session, I told her what I had experienced. Nothing seemed to resonate with her that is until I mentioned the sharp nose and ears is when she screamed hysterically only to confirm that she had seen this same image of a figure standing in her closet at night. The pictures that she had taken in her room did in fact portray what appeared to be a dark, short figure with pointy ears and a long sharp nose.

When she sent me copies of these photos I nearly fell out of my chair, it was something I never could figure would be so substantial even in a simple photograph.

It must have been nearly six to eight hours of speaking with "Jessica", along with countless exchanges of text messages to bring her solace, and a sense of guidance for her to be fully rid of these entities. When a person is under this kind of pressure, there are specific things I adamantly instruct the person that is being haunted to do, in order to bring up a solid barrier from the entities that are terrorizing the family and the home. If the person cannot follow the simple instructions I lay out for them within the course of at least three weeks, that is when I sit down with the person and ask them why they chose not to follow through with my counsel. And it was here, that we were nearly two weeks after her session, but I had found that "Jessica" had not followed through with my instructions. One of them being, to stop all communication with the entities entirely. Entities crave attention, and when you acknowledge the Demon's or a Familiar's presence that is when you're asking for the activity to only continue and worsen. I had taken much time and consideration into all areas of "Jessica's" case, however was faced with the unsettlingly reality that she had told me she didn't want to follow through with all of my advice. For instead of taking it upon herself to put up all barriers to protect her children and herself, she began to insinuate that there was no need to partake in the following instructions I presented to her to see that these entities left her premises. Instead she proceeded to believe that the power of prayer was more than enough.

Facing her choice, that was when I had to discontinue my services in helping her. Although I was articulate on the motivations and reasons behind my instructions, it's undoubtfully obvious that she was unwilling to fully be rid of these malicious pieces of existence. It was in "Jessica's" case that for the first time in my Demonology and Psychic Medium career, that I had to turn down a client from a haunting. Not in the slightest was I okay with this for it took over my whole conscience for weeks filled with guilt, wondering if I didn't do something right to fully convince her. But after a few weeks, I was reminded with the help of my Spirit Guides and Angels that there are going to be people in this world that won't want to fully be rid of the Demon's wrath. And for the sake of my child's safety and my own, that was when I had to pull the plug. Granted I did all that I could, but it was inevitable that some people just won't want to be completely done with it.

It's in this experience that I want to relay with extreme caution, that no matter how much you may say out loud that you want the entity gone -won't happen unless it's what you truly desire. Spirits are not so easily fooled by your loose words, instead they read into the DNA of truth that is spoken not through verbalization, but through your deepest intentions. The entity is able to fully read you as if your entire life, emotions, love, hate, fantasies, wonders, doubts, fears are written on paper. It doesn't take but an instant moment for the entity to fully be able to know whether or not you're done with absolute certainty. Although we discussed this earlier, it cannot be expressed enough, that the only way for the entity to be externally removed from one's life, must also be internally removed willfully.

⚠️

THE REMOVAL CLEANSING WARNING!

To compromise one's safety is when one is not willing to partake in all areas to properly extract that which isn't welcome with due haste. It is with this in mind, enables the entities full advantage if the person being targeted, isn't on board with all that must be done. And as contemporary or odd this next bit may appear to those new to these tips and techniques, I can speak with full confidence that these do work -as long as one is following the cleansing guidelines most definitely.

However, to extend this cosmic truth, there are absolutely ***no guarantees*** that the entities haunting you won't still attempt to haunt, or terrorize you or your loved ones during this time. To understand, once the cleansing process goes into motion, there may or will be an exceptionally discouraged force that will fight back without mercy. For these Demonic forces don't go down without a fight and will persist with much effort in hopes to kick you back into the position of helplessness. Demons and Familiar Spirits are not and should not, under any circumstances, be challenged, or dared in any means. It is those that proceed to do so that only are left with a spiritual and even physical bruising not too long after the fact. These are lively, supernatural opponents that crave altercations, and will only encourage this through motivation and further fear. The moment a person begins to harass or dare an entity to show them their power, is a person that will most quickly regret this moment indeed.

Those that confront the Spirits will be faced with a damaged pride and must reluctantly seek Spiritual counsel if they want the situation handled as soon as possible. For once the entity has been challenged, that rage will be expressed through the use of external force. Whether this force is expressed by throwing objects, or hurting people, that force can be amplified to a degree that not even the most highly of trained officials could justly imagine.

It is here that I urge with a sincere heart, to think before one acts in anger towards these types of Spirits. They may be invisible, but they are not impossible to be fully felt through the motivation of fear and ultimate hatred.

REMOVAL CLEANSINGS AND SEALING TECHNIQUES

To fully remove an unfriendly entity, there are several guidelines I instruct in order for the peace to return with the home and within one's essence. However, if any of these tips are not done with maximum intention, then the entity will continue to reside and haunt your home. The list below is organized based on the need of necessity, so as to remove the entity(s) most successfully. Each tip in cleansing and sealing cover areas in a physical, mental, and a Spiritual (Psychic) sense of protection. All of these focused areas ***must*** be completed in order to see a change in one's sense of self and home. There will also be a detailed instruction on how often the cleansing, or sealing must be performed, in order to bring back order, peace and tranquility into yourself and the home.

PRAYER

The power of prayer is by far one of the number one things that must be taken place when in any kind of Spiritual warfare. For those of the Ascended Realms on the Other Side will stop at nothing to assist you in your journey without obligation or hesitation. The overpowering love from Angels, Ascended Masters like Jesus Christ, Buddha, and others from the many faiths, are forever here to guide and protect you in the name of love. Regardless of your faith, even if nonreligious, they're not going to leave you alone in this fight and will be there to guide and protect you along the way. It's important to remember that there is only so much these brilliant guides can do, for the purest gateway from these dark times is if we allow it to continue to consume our very light. They're our guides, indeed to protect, but they're also here to teach us the skills by providing us with the tools on just how to do so with courage and faith within ourselves. Don't hesitate to ask upon those in the light to help you during the difficult time whenever you need, and be very specific of what it is you are requesting.

-TIME OF NEED: As soon as possible when feeling threatened. As often as one feels is necessary, such as once awakening from sleep or before falling asleep.

REMOVE OBJECTS AND EMPTY DEVICES

Spirits enter our lives through nearly countless of ways, but if the entity were to enter through an empty device such as a Ouija Board then it is crucial for the board to be burned out of the home immediately. The sooner the board is burned the better the chances of closing the doors that were once opened. Granted, the Psychic door is still opened and will require further steps to close them, but by burning the Ouija Board it prevents the entities from continuing communication through that device. This will also ensure that no one else in the home is tempted to partake in further communication.

This would include if the person used anything that were resonating with the occult or dark magic. Which would include items from Witchcraft, candles, Wicca items (if spells were casted), Voodoo, Hoodoo, Satanism devices and anything else that was derived or targeted towards a negative aspect in open communication with entities and the Other Side. Even if those objects were no longer used but were to remain in the home, the entities that were drawn with the use of those items - whatever they were, no matter how minimal they may seem - must be removed. This also includes attire, such as any ceremonial clothing that may have been worn during a conjuring, spell casting, or even if that was what you wore for the sake of that particular Spiritual practice. All items, and I mean *all items* that were used for the use of occult must be removed with great haste.

To remove these types of items, so as to ensure that no other person is also set with this same terrible fate, must also be burned. However, if you wish to not burn the items, such as the clothing, or whatever else, then it would be necessary to do the following cleansing.

-TIME OF NEED: As soon as possible! However, once these items have been burned, then once. But if desired to keep the remaining items, or choose to donate them, they must be cleansed thoroughly before hand, or for the remaining days kept within the home.

SAGE, SAGE, SAGE!

Sage is one of the oldest and most respected Spiritual techniques used to cast out diabolic forces. The burning of Sage has been used by, Native Americans for thousands of years, and is one of the most effective natural tools that will work for nearly every situation -including Demons and Devils.

To use Sage, you would take the bundle of Sage and burn it either when it's still wrapped within it's bundle, or by breaking it into pieces and burning it onto a safe surface. Once the Sage has been lit, it will burn similar to an incense stick. As the smoke fills the air, take either your hand or a feather of your choice, and waft the smoke onto yourself to cleanse your own energy vibration. Cleansing yourself with Sage only takes a few moments, which is then when you can continue your cleansing by wafting the remaining smoke within the home.

When cleansing and sealing your home with Sage, it's advisable to recite your own prayer that is clear in your intentions of the cleansing. The prayer is best to be spoken with assertiveness, love, courage, and full intent without doubt. There are no better prayers than what is most suitable for you. However, if you don't know of a prayer, or not sure what to say when saging your home, and yourself, this prayer below would be most effective. It's a personal cleansing speech I recite each time I begin my own cleansings and it's not failed me yet:

"Only love, light and positive energy may reside here. All negative entities that are not welcome must leave in the name of love. No negatively charged entity may cross this barrier. I call upon positive, and loving Ascended souls to assist in my sealing and protection of I, and my family.
Thank you."

SPIRITUAL NOTE

When you begin your Sage cleansing, it's advisable to begin in your bedroom and then continue *outward* towards the rest of the house. This will initialize the cleansing barrier to start from the inside, and pushing the entity out of the home/ location. The tip is, to start from the *inside and working your way out of the house.* People that start from outside and then cleanse to the inside of the house end up doing what's called a **Spirit**

Lockdown. Which will ultimately lock and trap the entity inside your home and anger the Spirit further.

If for any reason you think you may have accidentally trapped a Spirit in your residence, it would be wise to seek immediate Spiritual counsel for further individual instruction. But until you can do so, you could attempt to reverse this by attempting the proper cleansing in the way that's instructed by also verbalizing to the entities that they are free to go.

-TIME OF NEED: One must be aware that Sage is not a cleansing that is set in stone. The cleansing is similar to what I call, a *Spirit Repellant.* It only works for a few weeks then begins to wear off, which is why I suggest to those dealing with Spiritual attacks or in the dealings of a severe haunting to Sage at least once a week.

However, if you're a person that is a Lightworker, Empath, Psychic Medium, or any other type of Spiritual Catalyst, then it would be wise to Sage your residence for the rest of your physical days on this planet. Reason being is because those of that type of Spiritual life, mission, are most likely to be continually followed and attached from negatively charged Spirits. Saging your home and yourself as often as once a week or twice a month will ensure the continual metaphysical safety and peace.

SALT SEALING

The use of salt is exceptional for the properties in salt bring a positive vibration back into the very property of your home and space. When using salt, it's best to sprinkle the salt around your entire home either in a thin or thick line, so as to create an energetic barrier of protection. Many presume this to be something of White magic, personally I've not felt this way about salt for we eat salt everyday, which is one of the major reasons as to why it's so helpful. The purpose of salt is to initiate a barrier of protection in order to instruct a cosmic energy field similar to like an aura. However, this energy field cannot be created without your belief that it is done through your consciousness in deciding it so. So truth be told, this can be done with any type of salt as long as your soul vibration is sparking with the fullest intent to create this energetic barrier. For it is in the belief that assists in the motion of the sealing itself.

The other form of salt sealing that I highly recommend is by circulating salt around your bed in a thick or thin line. This sealing will allow you a greater advantage so as to keep negative Spirits from sitting on top, or under you while you're asleep. For dark entities like to attack living people in their sleep while intercepting into the person's third eye. With this sealing it will construct a helpful barrier similar to that of a dome around your entire bed.

Salt barriers can also be done at the doors of your bedroom and window sills. Here the sealing would ensure that entities cannot come through the door ways, including negatively charged living people that intend harm on you or your family which helps in finding who is your enemy or your ally.

-TIME OF NEED: A salt barrier sealing must be done at least once every few months. The moment activity persists, that is when the salt sealing should be done again so as to ensure further safety. If suspecting of being physically, or psychicly attacked during your sleep, *now* would be the time to perform this sealing.

WHITE CANDLES

The burning of a white candle lifts the energies in the atmosphere that which encourages further positive energy to overtake the room and space. Those of a negative energy are drawn to negative intentions, whereas the white candle is the color meaning for purity, holiness, love, and divine security and truth. Some people believe that if you use a candle, that it's best to use one that was blessed by a holy person or by the power a prayer, which is equally helpful when bestowing positive vibrations.

-TIME OF NEED: Whenever you may feel insecure in your safety, take a white candle and begin burning it in the room that which you feel needs it most. However, if the candle doesn't burn, or something strange happens that prevents you from burning the candle or any other candles, this may be a Spiritual indicator that you could be in the presence of an unhappy Spirit. If this occurs, begin the Sage cleansing as soon as possible, followed with prayer.

SPIRITUAL NOTE

It's inadvisable to use candles that are red or black. Candles that are red, many are told it's the sign of love but what I've learned overtime that it most often is the sign of blood and physical harm. For those that have used these candles, especially during occult ceremonial practices have endured heavy penalties. The color black is also commonly believed to help secure the person's safety -but I can tell you that's incredibly false and mustn't be used under any circumstances. If you've ever used these candles and have undergone Spiritual attacks, it would be wise to throw the candles away as soon as possible.

DISASSOCIATE WITH THOSE OF RISK

It's advisable to immediately disassociate with anyone that may be in the means of dark Spiritual practices for your own safety and wellbeing. No matter how long you've known someone, sometimes no matter how much you may love them, they may have to be set aside for your own good. Talking with the person(s) that are suspect of these types of risky practices would allow a chance at a possible even ground with them. However, if you cannot come up with an agreement for all concerned, then it's best to end ties completely.

The reason for ending this type of bond, is due to the fact that when you associate with someone that has a negative Spirit attached to them, that same entity will begin to become attached to *you* also. To ensure you are not at risk, the lengths of disconnecting from a person for your own safety may come as a life necessity.

-TIME OF NEED: Do so when you feel it is absolutely necessary.

OLIVE OIL

The use of olive oil helps in achieving a Spiritual barrier on your body. This is where you are to take a dab of the oil from the tip of your forefinger, and placing the oil on your forehead, wrists, on the outside of your ankles, above the navel, and on your lower back just above the buttock. By doing this, the entity is forbidden to touch your temporary physicality. The placement of the olive oil on your forehead is exceptionally important for this protects your third eye from being tainted or tarnished by malicious forces. It also ensures you're not altered in any way while you are in sleep state. Any kind of olive oil is fine to use for this type of cleansing. Some may also prefer to motion the olive oil in the shape of a cross when dabbing it along the skin, which is also very effective if desired. All that matters, is the protection is done to protect you and your loved ones from physical touch.

-TIME OF NEED: It's best to do right before bedtime at least once a month or when feeling necessary. If you're being physically attacked however, now would be the time to do so once a week for an entire month.

LEAVE THE RESIDENCE OR LOCATION

In order to remain as safe as possible is to decide whether it's necessary to leave the premises for good. For those that may have recently moved to a new home only to discover the Paranormal disturbances started not too long after the arrival -then chances are the entity is attached to the location. If you were to move this may give you a chance at a normal life, but in order to be certain, would require the assistance and professional opinion from a Psychic Medium in your area. There are no guarantees that the entity won't follow you to your new location or home of choice, but I do encourage that it's always worth the try if you're desperate to seek peace back into your family's life.

However, if you're under the impression that the activity occurred due to you visiting a location that is known to be haunted, or wherever you feel it may have followed you from, it would be best to not return to that location again. And to proceed with using Sage to cleanse yourself and of your home by instructing the entity to leave in the name of love, while asking Angels to assist in this removal and sealing.

-TIME OF NEED: When you feel is necessary or if at all.

CRYSTALS

It would help when wearing certain crystals that permeate specific energetic vibrations that will further assist in Psychic protection. The list of helpful crystals is nearly endless for the protection properties are different and some are necessary more than others depending on what your greatest concerns are. There are some crystals that enable further protection in Psychic energy, where another crystal may embody enhanced emotional stability and physical safety. One that is known to be highly recommended is Black Tourmaline or others like it. I've found the stone Black Tourmaline to be the most dominant when in need of preventing other entities or living people sucking your energetic vibrations. It's known to build a barrier of protection in order to allow you to remain secure in your Psychic energy and physicality.

-TIME OF NEED: Wear when feeling necessary.

HOLY WATER

The person can either acquire holy water from a local pastor from their church, or can easily be made from prayer in the privacy of your own home. Holy water doesn't have to be set as 'holy' by someone within a religious background but can be transformed as so by the power from your one's own personal belief through their own psychic energy. Holy water is better sprinkled on the persons that are being blessed followed with their own desired and comfortable prayers. The same can be done when blessing the person's home or personal space. Holy water can also be sprinkled upon objects one feels may be cursed or is a possible conduit.

-TIME OF NEED: As soon as the person begins to have Paranormal activity. Cleansing both the persons involved along with cleansing the home and outside location.

SEEKING SPIRITUAL COUNSEL

It's always best to remain humble in the reality that we don't always hold all the answers in these difficult matters, and sometimes it's helpful to seek guidance from others. Not all those that are Spiritual will be comfortable discussing the matters of a Paranormal disturbance however, and you've probably already come to discover this over time unfortunately. It's a fact that most people are greatly uncomfortable hearing or even talking about these types of metaphysical issues and would prefer to pretend it's not a cosmic reality. Keeping this in mind, it's best to remain aware that not all people in a Spiritual lifestyle, religion or practice are going to be open to helping you. This is where it would be necessary to seek those of a specific background/ career that is targeted towards assisting those of these troubling situations. Remembering to find those that have the fullest intention to helping you be rid of these entities and not entertain themselves by challenging the entity further. For those that say they'll help you, may in fact make it worse by doing a number of things that we've discussed prior that wouldn't be a wise. When seeking guidance from someone, make sure to also do your homework on who it is you're seeking guidance or assistance from. Don't be afraid to ask of their experience, for this is your life you're in concern of and as a professional this person should have no problem presenting their credibility. However, if the person is to become easily offended, and is unwilling to assist in presenting you with this kind of information, or seems to give you an unsure or uneasy feeling, then this would be the time to listen to your intuition, and discontinue their counsel, and move on to the next person.

Also, if they begin to ask you to pay for certain services that seem considerably costly then this person is only looking to make money and is not in consideration of your best interest. I cannot tell you how many clients have revealed to me how many Psychics and other types of Spiritual Counselors told them they needed to buy their products on a continual basis just to find peace in their home. I personally and professionally am disgusted and have no problem telling you that those people are frauds and are not doing this job for the concern nor care of your wellbeing, and mustn't be trusted. These types of people are going to tell you nearly every visit or meet, that you're attracting the entity -which can be true depending on the situation, but they're going to usually say this to every person they consult. If this turns out to be your situation with those that say they could help you, then I'd recommend you politely turn them down and move on to someone that you can trust and who isn't going to charge an arm, and a leg.

There's the widespread misconception that Exorcists are God's warriors when it comes to Demonology and assistance of Spiritual warfare, but even an Exorcist is going to charge for their services. It's not unusual for even your local church to charge a small or sometimes moderate fee when requested to see to a possible Paranormal disturbance. And most often thousands of those pleas are never answered for the fact that they simply cannot keep up with all of the requests. And ultimately are paid for just the persons requesting to be helped sadly, which is where it's not a service that should be paid for in my professional opinion.

And it's because of this that I do what I do free of charge. Think about it, how would you feel if you had a person break into your home, and for protection you call the local police department. The police show up at your home to protect and to serve, but then suddenly they shove a piece of paper in your face while saying, "We won't help until you pay us." Granted, the state pays for their honorary service for the safety of Americans, however it's also from the trust in the system in the matter that even if you don't have anything in your name, you're forever under the care and supervision of our police force. However, it's even known within the police force to have a few that are going to do things under the table, and even dishonor their very badge they wear. But it's because of those that do things for the good of others with love and respect, that uphold the very principals of our communities, year round.

Being a Demonologist is just like being a police officer but within a Spiritual and metaphysical sense. However, those that partake in this field may not always be so trustworthy, which is recommended to remain fully aware of who it is you choose to consult. Regardless, be sure it's someone that is going to make the situation better and not worse.

-TIME OF NEED: The moment one feels needs this type of help and or guidance.

IN JESUS' NAME

Respectfully it wouldn't be fair to partake in this chapter without adding J.C. into the mix. And as usual as this may sound, I implore you to take a moment to ponder on this portion respectfully.
The unfortunate truth is not always will Jesus Christ be there to save us from these kinds of situations. Not that his holiness won't, but that sometimes in certain situations his presence may not come to our rescue for reasons based on the need of the individual. Sometimes the person may not receive his help based on the need of the person discovering their own courage in handling the situation on their own. However, this doesn't mean his love isn't going to be there to wish you positive vibrations or the help that is required. As a Psychic Medium I've learned from Jesus (not being religious) that his presence is meant as a guide, not solely as a primary protector. As absurd as this may sound to those of a religious background, it's what

I've discovered after years of heavy Demonic Oppression of my own. It was through his guidance that allowed me to seek and find truth within myself on how to help myself, along with helping and guiding humanity humbly. There is no greater gift, than the gift of learning how to protect yourself. As many have heard of the saying:

Give a man a fish, he eats for a day, teach a man to fish, he eats for a lifetime.

Here is to articulate the relating concept to fish as the shield of knowledge of divine protection. If one were to slightly adjust the sentence in the manner below then it would gently guide one to a slightly wider perspective in the meaning of truth to divine protection:

Give a man a shield, he is saved for a day, teach a man to create his own shield then he is saved for a lifetime.

-TIME OF NEED: As often and as soon as one feels.

LOVE CONQUERS ALL

For one to be completely free from the bondage of hate and fear, one must uncover their innate cosmic courage that is fearless. In order for one to seek peace within, must internally seek this and discover the peace from within themselves. Though the bondage is external and is from conscious entities indeed, the truest and strongest form of bondage is the one we give ourselves. Your very existence lies within your hands and your hands alone. No person, and no other form of energy can change this. You're the one in control of yourself, of your decisions and of the moment you choose to release yourself from the cosmic battle that once enslaved even the most respected of holy men and women. The only way to discover how to withstand and defend thyself is by discovering the courage and the light warrior that once laid dormant. For it is now in this moment to awaken the soldier of love within to unveil the power from inside of your very soul.

It is no trickery, nor is it a mystical abomination but the energetic and cosmic DNA that was and always will be the truest form of power that can overcome even the darkest of foes. That power is in no need of acceptance of others but of acknowledgement of one's own personal truths. This power has no need to be in control of others, but in control of thyself for the only one that can change their present is to change the very concept one believes within themselves. This power isn't to be confused with weakness, for this power enables even the most underestimated to be the force that withstands and overcomes odds that appeared greater than them. This energy isn't something that has to be borrowed nor taken but is a power that is deep within the depths of the heart. That power is love. And it is through the power of love that conquers any obstacle despite the challenges that may lay ahead.

Here the person must dig deep with inside themselves to reveal the purity that was never tainted from the faults of the world, or tarnished from the negative imperfections of others.

An emotion embodying the intricate personality and character strengths of who you were always meant to be and to uphold. Love is neither dominating nor is it inferior but remains in the neutral state of awareness of the ultimate good. It is the emotion one feels from the loss of a love or when receiving a kiss from a crush. It is the state of being in the moment of serene presence that creates only beauty and wonder. It is in one's almighty birthright to take the wheel of self-doubt, and act into one's accord of Divine purpose for the highest good. We are not without love no matter the level of one's loneliness. For those that seek that which isn't physically there, may already possess what one is in seek of, and shall only discover this truth after searching from within thyself.

In the sake of humility, there is only you that enables or disables those that hold you bondage. It is from with inside yourself that drives the ultimate truth to reach to one's fullest potential without limits. And it is in these sorts of battles, either physical, metaphysical, emotional, or mental that can either brighten their Light or diminish it. No matter the ability of one's opponent, it is inside of your *being* that can either make or break your bondage. And it is in ourselves that either allows the wrath to overtake us in hopelessness, or to break beyond those limitations and unleash the light that is inside all of us.

As I lay in the darkness of the abyss of nothingness,
it is in this I discovered what I didn't desire.
Though my foe had defeated me in this battle,
I would not give into the war.
For thy power isn't based on what was given,
nor what was taken,
but what I believe to be my truth.
Love is not without feeling,
and feeling cannot be absorbed completely,
no matter how consumed into darkness I may be.
It is here, in this moment of darkness that I discovered that love
was my light to guide me out of my own defeat,
remembering what I always was and forever will be.

As long as you have love
you will always be guided back into the light.

The Making of Demons and Familiars

Where do I start?...

There is not a day that goes by where I'm not haunted by the memories of the countless Demonic experiences that I've had. Let's not forget to mention an unfortunate series of tremendously unfair atrocities of bad luck. None of these moments have *not* shaken my very soul from the closely unspeakable realities of these metaphysical beings. When I started this book, I knew that I was going to be in a whirlwind of Hell, however I was not so certain to what extent that would be. Soon enough I was awakened with shrilling moments that would trigger my deepest fears back to life.

It has been a little over a year since I decided to write a book such as this. When I made the internal decision, a chill ran down my spine, as if I knew through intuition, that all of the entities in the universe were suddenly made aware of this project. Little did I know they were *indeed* and were not happy about it to say the least.

To verbalize the experiences through a brief list would not justly describe the lengthy details for each moment holds it's own piece of cosmic dialogue. However, if I were to elaborate on the case of each, it would take far too many pages. So below, will be a brief list of the things that have happened to me since I started the making of *Demons & Familiars*. All that is written is true, and is not exaggerated nor adjusted for the need of special effects. Truth be told, I wish some *weren't* true, but they are, and it's what I'm haunted by each day. But,... if I were given a chance to change my mind in making this book, I'd still do it again though knowing what would lay ahead. For I believe in the purpose more than the turbulence during the journey..

- ✛ Two earthquakes occurred just after I started the first pages of this book. One scaling to a 7.1.
- ✛ Received bruises and scratch marks that I could not explain.
- ✛ Power outages occurred nearly three times when attempting to write.
- ✛ During typing my computer would somehow restart on its own or shut off without any explanation and destroying the last few pages I had written. I learned quickly to save *continuously.*
- ✛ Had countless Astral Realm attacks by Demons and Familiar Spirits.
- ✛ Had two lice outbreaks that had happened on my daughter. However, when I asked the school about the lice outbreak, no one reported having this happen to them. This is when I knew it was another Spiritual attack.
- ✛ My daughter was pushed down the stairs by an unseen force. She was only eight years old when this occurred.
- ✛ Excessively drained nearly every day when attempted to write more pages for this book. So drained that no

matter how much sleep I had, it was like I was slowly losing existence.

- Doors would open or close by themselves. I'd watch this happen in front of me during the day. There were no windows open, nor was anything able to debunk this happening.

- Experienced Psychic blows to the head when writing the book. It was as if someone was standing behind me and would hit my head with full aggression.

- Phone calls and phone would act strange. The phone would begin swiping to several pages as if someone was touching and using my cell phone. Nothing like that has ever happened before. Is it a coincidence that this also happened when I was talking to a friend about Demonic activity? *I think not.*

- A person had stolen money from my credit card by hacking into my private information, *twice. Which has never happened before.*

- Had terrible nightmares that were so lucid I'd wake up screaming and sweating in the middle of the night.

- I'd hear banging and scratching sounds next to my head in the middle of the night.

- Had a strange swarm of flies that began invading my home without explanation.

- I went to the bathroom around midnight, only to suddenly hear a child's voice say to me, *"Hi there.."*

- next to my head. Though this was a seemingly innocent childlike voice, I knew this was a Demon in disguise for I could feel it's vile energetic vibration.
- I had woken up to something pulling my legs at night that was an invisible force.
- I went to a bar with a friend and after the bar closed my friend and I attempted to walk a man to his home. After spending a few hours with the man, he insisted we take a drink with him. To skip all the details, the man drugged both my friend and I and the man we helped, raped me.

During the rape I had an Astral Projection experience where I found myself with my Twin Flame that passed away in 2012. He and other souls told me the reason this was happening was because Demon's overtook this man's body and drove him to assault me in hopes to stop me from continuing the book. I didn't believe it until I asked to see it for myself. As hard as this sight was, I was awakened with the harsh reality that I was witnessing over one hundred Demons jumping into this man's body to get their chance at assaulting my physicality. There was seemed to be an endless line of Demons and even negatively charged Earth Bound souls waiting in a line like I was suddenly a ride at the state fair.

Hard to believe? I don't blame you. Yet that's the truth. I don't consider the fear or the concern for possible judgment, but to help you explore just how dedicated these monsters can become. There is no mercy in these entities and there is no sense in trying to reason with them, for their very concept and purpose to existence is to cause fear and harm.

After the rape, I'd developed new triggers that I hadn't had before. Fears of being in certain public places and unable to function in certain situations or conversations that arose. However, the healing process has indeed been a long and strenuous one, but the journey wasn't over. The book was only half way through at the time, and it took nearly three months to start up and write again. I was close to giving up, so close that I nearly picked up my computer and threw it against the wall. I had envisioned the act for weeks. Breaking the very thing that created another version of Hell in my mind. Forget my body. This was no longer a war in my temporary chalice, but within the pedestal of my very conscience that held the desire to continue for the sake of mankind.

"How could I continue after this? What was the point? It's not like people will believe me. What difference is this going to make anyways? What else could I accomplish, especially when I felt already defeated during the making. I hadn't been anyone special. No one usually takes me seriously, so what point would it be to attempt to stop me from making such a book...?"

These were the many questions that would continue to roll around within my inner dialogue. Questioning the very point to why these Demons would go to such a length. For the very idea didn't make sense due to not seeing the cosmic threat that apparently, I surely was.

After a few more weeks I was able to begin writing again. Though I was reluctant, I knew that the only way I could overcome my own fears was by forcing my way through. As the pages began to unfold, so were the Demon's next move. Within a few nights I began to have several nightmares, and lucid experiences where I felt as if I were in terrorizing traps that I couldn't get out of. Although I was aware these were dreams, I was still aware that even in our dreams, can become the reality that we may not be able to withstand.

For the next thing I know I had found myself in a dream experience where I had was sitting on the lap of my Twin Flame. What seemed like a dream come true to finally express my love in a higher dimension, this fairy tale rapidly developed into my worst nightmare. As I gazed upon the eyes that I've loved the moment I've witnessed them, in a matter of seconds I suddenly felt my consciousness being shaken and pulled out of this experience against my will. Once this Psychic pull stopped, I found myself still with my friend. However, as I had a looked at him, I realized with my discernment that I was no longer with my Twin Flame. The person I was now sitting on was *something* else.

The face of this person was unlike something I've ever witnessed before. His very smile it revealed was unwaveringly chilling. His eyes were like daggers as the pupils pulsed to a degree that not even humanity could dare imagine. Trying to remain calm, I told myself to keep cool and to not react. It didn't take long for me to realize I had been suddenly Psychicly placed into a trap that I couldn't get out of. Similar to that of a trance that was unlike anything I've experienced, and I had no idea how I was going to get out of it. When people ask *how* I know what Demons and Devils can do -it's because of these experiences.

Slowly leaning back from this man that was no longer my friend, I asked *it* who *it* was. As it spoke, the very vibration of it's words were unwelcoming. How can I truly explain what this experience was like? It was like I was sitting on the lap of the Devil. The pressure and power it had was menacing, overpowering and wasn't an opponent I had ever faced before. As I attempted to get away from this metaphysical stranger, it pinned me down against my will and began to rape me. How can I tell you what this was like? It was like being stripped of your dignity and torn with thousands of sharpened knives. It wasn't pleasant and was degrading to say the least. The very weight of this thing was as if hundreds of pounds were on top of me, and the only thing I was left to do was cry. The pain was nothing short of excruciating. It was as if my entire insides were being pureed with only leaving what was left of my anguish. I remember doing the best I could to think of the love I had with my daughters. If it wasn't for thinking of them, I don't know how I would've held on.

Yes, this was a dream, but it was the most horrifying and painful nightmare I've ever endured. Those that are shamed over these kinds of traumatic occurrences are not to be misunderstood, for their very will to continue is a marvel of its own.

The next thing I remember is recalling that vanity is the best medicine for distraction. Attempting to flatter such a thing was difficult as I tried to find ways to insinuate its existence in a manner that was less than disturbing. Although difficult, it had worked for then it became intrigued from my flattery. In any case, this was a generous strategy that saved my endurance. As it stopped the sexual assault, it began to ask me what I liked the most about it. While the entity slowly loosened its grip upon my body, there was an instance that still haunts me. For as I was staring off into the mindless space of nothingness from the pain, I was awakened back into a daunting reality from the slick and wisp of a tail now grazing along my chin. Nearly memorized, I regained conscience once the sight of the intricate details of the tail's scales began to catch my undivided attention.

In adding to its variety of impressive abilities, I proceeded to express admiration for its power to construct such a scheme of manipulation. Here the entity and I locked eyes and it's a moment I'll never forget. Though it still possessed the face of my friend, it's very depths were like daggers of infinite despair. As if piercing into my soul with the fullest intent to counter what it was opposite of. It was here where I asked *it* the monumental question that I knew would guide me to the answers to where and why this was happening.

Me: "..Can I ask you a question.?"

Entity: "Yeah, ..go ahead."

Me: "What are you?"

Entity: ".. I am called many things."

Me: "Are you.. the Devil?.."

Entity: "You could say that. Some call me Diablo, Heaven's Fallen Angel, Lucifer, Satan..."
Here it began to speak in several different languages in attempts to continue to describe its presence.

Me: "But, .. it says in religion that you are most often portrayed as a beautiful-

Devil: "-Beautiful blonde guy that has blue eyes. Yeah, I've heard this story a shit load of times -*why?* Do you want to see me that way? *Will that turn you on?*"

Me: "Well, I am curious to see what you can do.."
Again, trying to bait it with flattery in hopes to distract it from hurting me.

It was in this moment the entity that claimed to be a Devil transformed its entirety in front of my very eyes. I watched as it changed from a grotesque walking, talking grunge to now an exceptionally impressive and, dare I say, extremely attractive species of a man. However, though his physical appearance was the intent to falsify even myself, the Devil's energy was too vulgar to upkeep with the holy camouflage. Observing the deliverance for it's attempt, but watched as the very gold on it's body began to fade into a misty dust that slowly swayed away from the not so talented magician.

Taken back by the wake of this master deceiver's capabilities, that was when I began to sway away in hopes to find a way out. But the entity was too fast. For the moment I managed to take even a few steps from it's magnificence fierceness, I was pinned down yet a second time. A fear began generating inside of me as this powerhouse of darkness catapulted a range of strikes against my very will. I felt outnumbered as this Master foe shapeshifted into what I can only identify as a monster that was from the depths of my deepest fears. Hideous for the sight of it only groomed the ugliest ideas and atrocities that roamed within my consciousness. Black as the pit of night while accompanied with the smell of something like the walking dead. But the company wasn't completed without its own pores birthing what appeared to be miniature creatures that only formed further abominations. The latter of evil only escalated to extricate more fear in order to achieve the ultimate goal. As the menacing battle to fight for my very existence continued, so did the spawn of the evil.

Once they had me where they wanted, weak and unable to fight, that was when the once dashing apprentice pressed its now flattering claws onto my third eye and again pulled me to what was now another dimensional trap. Severally damaged, left with uncertainty, I began to see the collision of what seemed to be thousands of Demons surround me in this float abys of nothingness. Being pulled, and tarnished by countless claws, it was here where I realized I was witnessing the undoubted experience of one's lifetime and of one's nightmare.

The reality that these Demons could see and speak to me directly. It was in this soul shaking instance where I could hear through Telepathy all of their anger, hatred, and gut-wrenching desires to do further unspeakable damage to my Spirit.

Hearing as one said, "She's the bitch that's going to ruin us!" Recalling the agenda as another said, "Let's all have at her!" It was like being now laid out as the toy that they always wanted. This my dear reader, wasn't something I ever imagined would happen. Even to me.

As I now appeared to be playing the role of an empty device they wanted to penetrate, I was faced with unstable yet silent despair that seemed oh so sweet. Suddenly, I was okay with not wanting to be alive, or to even exist at all. The very idea of being no longer in existence felt desirable, even similar to that of a sexual fantasy that I craved. It was so tantalizing that the very concept triggered me. I could hear within my own echo of silence that seemed to loom over me a voice however. And it was the voice that might as well have been God.

Here, I heard the voice of my Twin Flame call to me saying,

"Melinda -I'm going to get you out! Hold on!"

It was the voice that might as well be the definition of love itself. His love was what drastically shook me back from this menacing doom and rocked me back to the reality that I had to escape. Blasted back into awareness, that was when I gazed in the shuttering truth that the only person that was going to get me out was me. Though I had attempted to call for God's help, thinking this was what could rescue me, truth be told no one came. Not sure why this was, I knew the only way to escape was if I infiltrated my own energy to produce enough life back into myself. And it was here, where I focused within and made to motion, to remember all of those that I loved, and that loved me. Recalling the laughter of my daughters. Remembering the memories from my life, and with those that I had come to earth for. It was here I created energy, a light from within myself that drove the thousands of Demons to hide in fear. For I was no longer in fear, but was in complete control of taking back my balance, peace, and love for myself.

Somehow, once this occurred, I was able to zap back into my first dimensional trap where the Devil was still on top of me. Once I returned, it was in this exact purpose where I consciously manifested a dagger into my hands and stabbed the entity causing it to back off with tremendous impulse. As the blade engaged into the Descended Master's side, I hastened my way toward what appeared to be a door to my escape. But to my fear, the door was locked. Here I felt doom yet again. Feeling defeated, unsure of what else to do or where to go. And as I breathed in my fate, I heard the malicious entity's laugh. Ripping the dagger out of it's side with rage, the entity peered my way and said,

> **Devil:** "..What's the matter Melinda? Guna go write that fucking book of yours?"

It was in this very moment my heart dropped and the knowing now became clear. All of this was because of my book. However, confused as to how, or why my book would be such a threat, I proceeded to answer the Devil's question.

Me: "So that's what all of this is about.. Yes. It's going to help a lot of people."

Devil: "Do you think that book is going to stop me and my race?!"

Me: "I'm not trying to stop you from anything, but I am trying to help others from becoming your next victims. As powerful as you are, and as much as I respect that of you, I will continue to write this book if it's the last thing I do."

Devil: "You talk as if you know what fear is. You speak of fear as if you know how powerful it is.. You haven't seen nothing yet.."

As the Devil spoke, I slowly started sliding towards my next attempt at escape, for the next door was only a few feet away. Though as determined as my attempt to escape was, the Devil was faster, bigger, and grander in scale that I've never witnessed before. As it's size grew so did the level of intimidation and fear. And even though I was able to overcome the fear from the thousands of lesser powerful Demons, I was no match for the Descended Master. For I was only a foot away from grasping the next attempt at escape, only to feel it's towering monster claws jab into my waist, slaying me back to the position of helplessness once again. Begging for a sign that I'd be able to regain ability to see the light of hope again, was when I now plummeted towards my defeat. But it wasn't until the menacing face of the overgrown abomination motioned it's mutilated copy of my friend's face into mine -was when I just remember screaming beyond my own comprehension from utter belief that I was a goner.

But it was suddenly in this instance where out of a bright light my Twin Flame came to me as fast as the speed of light to rescue me. The feeling of being in his arms was something sweeter than I can describe. There's no safer sense of security than knowing that his love was there to save me from what I had endured. But he was not without the help of other Ascended Light beings that came and blasted the entity back into the universe.

These experiences were real, as real as you are reading this now. The moral of this experience, was learning that no matter what one is in, you're always given a chance to remember who you truly are. And as long as you continue to fight for what you believe in, then you'll be guided back to the source of your Light. When in doubt, love will guide the way, back into your deepest truths, desires and back into the way of what is good. And as long as you continue through despite the odds against you, you'll forever be guided and protected through the Spiritual warfare by other sources of love that too love you.

Acknowledgements

I want to thank all of those that supported and guided me here and from the Other Side, including my beloved Twin Flame. Without your supreme unconditional love and belief in me, I wouldn't have been able to accomplish this project. *Thank you* doesn't justly express how appreciative I am for all that you've done for me.

About The Author

Melinda Kay Lyons was born in Anchorage, Alaska and raised in the Last Frontier for a majority of her life. She is a proud mother of two daughters. Melinda does not align herself with religion, but is in ultimate faith of the power of the universe, Spirit and Source of love.

As her years stretched after her near-death experience, so did her intuitiveness and divine abilities as a Psychic Medium. Thanks to many positive influences, and pushes in the right direction, her dream of healing others has become a reality.

As a *Lightworker,* and *Psychic Medium* -Medium first, Psychic second -Melinda has helped people from her home state to the lower 48. With more than 12 years of Paranormal experiences, and a higher level of awareness of Spirit, her developed relationship with the respect and understanding of the afterlife has changed the lives of many.

Melinda has been a guest on a radio shows through iHeart Radio. She also is a host and daily vlogger on her official YouTube channel, where she goes within the depths of the Other Side while doing readings for clients. Reaching over 3 million people worldwide has not only humbled her but greatly increased in her desire to pursue her passion to enlighten and help others in the paranormal field. As a Demonologist, it's her not only a passion but her soul purpose to help those that may be dealing with a genuine haunting from unkind Spirits, which is why she offers this option completely free on her website.

Also By
Melinda Kay Lyons

WWW.LASTFRONTIERMEDIUM.COM

In DEMON DEALER, Lyons gives an in-depth look of what its like getting up close and personal with departed human souls, familiar spirits and deep into the gruesome Demon and Devil experience. Exploring mild paranormal occurrences like doors opening, full body apparitions, unexplained bangs, scratching noises, nightmares but quickly evolving into a more sinister journey.

Available for purchase at Amazon.com

Printed in Great Britain
by Amazon